MY SOARROARity™ RULES

MY SOARROARity™ RULES

A Sisterhood of Common Ground Among
12 Women and Their Rules of Restoration On the Rise

TONI T. ELLIS

MY SOARROARITY™ RULES
Published by Purposely Created Publishing Group™
Copyright © 2017 Toni Ellis

All rights reserved.

No part of this book may be reproduced, distributed or transmitted in any form by any means, graphics, electronics, or mechanical, including photocopy, recording, taping, or by any information storage or retrieval system, without permission in writing from the publisher, except in the case of reprints in the context of reviews, quotes, or references.

Unless otherwise indicated, scripture quotations are from the Holy Bible, King James Version. All rights reserved.

Scriptures marked NKJV are taken from the New King James Version®. Copyright © 1982 by Thomas Nelson. All rights reserved.

Printed in the United States of America

ISBN: 978-1-947054-32-5

Special discounts are available on bulk quantity purchases by book clubs, associations and special interest groups. For details email: sales@publishyourgift.com or call (888) 949-6228.

For information logon to:
www.PublishYourGift.com

This book is dedicated to Brenda Joyce Hickman. Before she was a nurse, wife, and mother, Brenda was a writer, scholar, and brilliant mind of her time. She wrote but was never published. Much of what was written will never be read by the masses.

I'm her eldest child. Now, I write. Thank you for preparing the way. Thank you for sharing your gifts. Thank you for writing on the pages of my little heart and teaching me to tell my story in my own words without trepidation.

CONTENTS

Acknowledgments 1

Foreword 3

Toni T. Ellis
EIGHTEEN YEARS AND ONE DAY 7

Deanna Cummings
NO LONGER CAPTIVE 19

Ronda Bailey
**FROM A SHAMEFUL PAST TO
A VICTORIOUS DESTINY** 33

Jocelyn L. Wallace
THE MIDDLE PASSAGE OF MY NAME 51

LaShonda Mobley
YOU ARE DESTINY'S CHILD 67

Tamara Omondi
BLOOMING WHILE BARREN 81

Kindra Lowery
THE INCARCERATION OF INVISIBILITY 95

Ashley Q. Tillman
DETERMINED DESPITE DOUBT 109

Tianna R. Lewis
BEING IS BELIEVING 121

Aisha Marshall
GREEN 137

Tosha Rone
THE HUXTABLE EFFECT 151

Shardé Edwards-Davis
THE POWER OF VULNERABILITY 165

About the Authors 181

ACKNOWLEDGMENTS

I give all praise, honor, and glory to God, Our Creator. I can do nothing without Him. He has opened every window and door, and poured out so many blessings. He equipped me to be in this position of empowering women to share their transformative messages in the form of books. I am because He is. I do because He does. I will because He can. My God has supplied every need and provided more than enough to continue this work. He has granted countless desires of my heart. I will forever seek Him first. Thank you Father, Son, and Holy Ghost.

To the coauthors of this first volume: I thank you for trusting me with your hearts. You shared, unashamed and unfettered. Your genuine willingness to be transparent will set many free from the bondage of isolation. Through your stories, every reader will see that they are not alone. I am eternally grateful for your investment in the futures of women all over the globe.

My humble husband: You would not let me quit; for that, I will always adore you. Thank you for making yourself and your treasures available to me and the people I serve. Through your selfless acts of kindness and endless sowing of seeds in all forms, many are helped. You make me smile, and my heart is happy because you are a part of my everyday life.

To every person who had a hand in the birthing process of this literary gift: I thank you for your time, attention to detail, and efforts in making this a smooth and pleasant production. We have more work to do and we pray that we can work with you again. Our joint efforts resulted in something extraordinary. The world could use more creative collaborations that produce what is promised.

Peace and Many Blessings!

Much Love!

FOREWORD

> "The abundant life does not come to those who have had a lot of obstacles removed from their path by others. It develops from within and is rooted in strong mental and moral fiber."
>
> —*William Mather Lewis*

Most women join a sorority because of its rich history and the impact the founding members had on communities throughout the world. When pledging a sorority, members gain a profound understanding of the organization's history and learn the importance of withstanding and surviving the toughest challenges in an individual's path, all while remaining committed to the organization's mission. Pledges go through the pledging process with a select group of women who are referred to as sisters, which encourages the strengthening of bonds. Sisters are there to provide strength when one feels weak or unable to withstand obstacles during the introductory phase of becoming a sorority sister.

Years ago, when I pledged my sorority, I was fortunate to foster long-lasting relationships with women who offered me valuable support from different perspectives. It's an unwavering bond that cannot be described. Even today, some of the women of my sisterhood continue to show me kindness and give me strength. They give me refuge when I am weak and afraid, and challenge me to change and be a better person. Most importantly they offer inspiration for the woman I continue to aspire to become.

Twelve women pledged a SOARROARity™ when they scribed together their personal life journeys on paper. Their service to all mankind is elegantly written throughout the chapters in this book. Their SOARROARity™ is very similar to a traditional sorority. However, unlike in a regular sorority where women may feel the need to hide their pain, these authors openly unmask the trauma, abuse, and illnesses that once hindered progression in their lives. These twelve women showed up, owned up, and acted up in order to rise up to the ordained occasion. They stretched each other. They cried together. They grew together. They shared their deep-rooted issues and experiences that caused unexpected setbacks in their lives. Furthermore, through shared bonds and the help of one another, these women have become more prepared to handle whatever else is ahead.

The outcome of the pledging process is unique but its true mission is to inspire and uplift other women's souls. In today's times, women are faced with much chaos, disorder, and stress that can affect their overall health, mentally, physically, and spiritually. After all, stress is a contributing factor to high blood pressure, heart disease, obesity, and diabetes.

We as wives, grandmothers, mothers, daughters, aunts, sisters, and friends must help each other find the essential tools to live stress-free to the best of our abilities. This is not an easy task, but it can be learned through shared experiences.

You will regain peace, clarity, and inspiration through each of these transformational testimonies. Every author will describe how you too can overcome any obstacle you may face throughout your journey in life. *My SOARROARity™ Rules* will guide you to a truth that will set you free and empower you to be restored to healing and wholeness. Enjoy the true-life stories this SOARROARity™ has so gracefully shared and gain the motivation to pursue your dreams of soaring.

LaShannon Spencer

TONI T. ELLIS

EIGHTEEN YEARS AND ONE DAY
My Mother, My Sister, My Friend

"Do not be offended by what God is going to allow."

Those words were spoken to me by someone I didn't even know. She was the pastor of a church in Nashville, Tennessee. I was visiting my sister in order to escape the woes of going through a tumultuous divorce. As a way of cheering me up, my sister took me to the movies. On the way home, we ended up stranded on the side of the road due to a minor accident that resulted in car troubles. The pastor rescued us from the dismal and dark highway in the middle of the night. On the ride home, my sister shared part of my sad story with this wisdom-filled woman of God. She said those words: "Do not be offended by what God is going to allow." Her response to my pain was not only confusing at the time, but felt as though she was dismissing my heartbreak.

When someone tells you not to be offended, most times, the natural inclination is to be offended. How many times have you been hurt to the core and someone suggests that you not take offense? How often have you heard that you were too sensitive? Have you been told that God has allowed something horrific to turn your life upside down? Has someone seemingly trivialized your personal tragedy as a God-ordained test?

On the flight returning to Las Vegas, I replayed in my mind the encounter with the pastor. In my heart, I knew this to be sound counsel. I knew the enemy wanted me to remain in a constant state of turmoil: Confused about God's will for my life, perplexed by the unplanned transition, confounded by the uncertainty of life. So from that point forward, I began to embrace that statement as a mantra to live by.

I survived the divorce. I thrived in my faith as a result of the restoration that soon followed. The advice offered during that particularly dark time proved to carry me through many more of life's disappointments. It was simply the best counsel I'd ever received in reference to coping with things that were out of my control. In fact, it left such a huge impact that I decided to share the powerful statement with my mother. She immediately embraced it as words to live by. Thereafter, whenever I was going through some type of rough patch in life, she would say, "Remember what the pastor told you, Tonia. Do not be offended by what God is going to allow."

While writing this book, my mother died. It was sudden. It was unexpected. It was preventable. Why now? Why her? Why me? Why, God? I was devastated. Sudden death, especially that of a parent, is an insurmountable challenge that pushes out all logic. It challenges your faith, your resilience, and your existence. And when there are unresolved issues between you and the loved one who left…it challenges your peace.

Psalm 119:165 proclaims, "Great peace have they which love thy law and nothing shall offend them." I was once again reminded that if I was to hold onto my peace, I am not to be offended by what God is going to allow.

There were only eighteen years and one day separating my mother and me in age. She was born September 7 and mine is September 8. She and my father married on December 25, 1968, when she was a senior in high school. I was conceived on their wedding night. My mother was married and pregnant while attending her last year of high school and still managed to graduate at the top of her class. Unfortunately, she was not permitted to carry out her duties as valedictorian, simply because she was carrying me. I believe this was the initial planting of her seed of resentment towards me. I do not believe it was intentional, but as offenses involving me were launched against her, the resentment grew uncontrollably.

Marriages between young people are prone to premature problems. My parents were no different. However, their issues were magnified by my father's violent and abusive ways. When my parents separated, my mother left because of his sexual abuse towards me. This became a huge source of pain that she never quite reckoned with and it divided us in ways that prevented us from genuine reconciliation. The perplexity of sexual dysfunction lending to a strained mother-daughter relationship is riddled with unnatural resentment.

Our relationship suffered the fallout of unintentional bitterness that began at my conception. It wasn't her fault. It wasn't my fault. It wasn't even my father's fault. We all suffered because the pain was generational. Their mutual dysfunction drew my parents together and eventually destroyed their dynamic and definition of love.

Is this scenario familiar to you? Can you attest to the fact that some of the brokenness you endure with family members is a result of generational dysfunction? Are you in a stuck place due to unresolved resentment that did not begin with you?

As the eldest child, I witnessed my mother's transformation from sheer joy to unbearable internal anguish. I listened to her vent and watched her cyclic depression. I called ambulances during panic attacks. I rubbed her back to soothe her nerves. I was her daughter, her sister, and her friend. This ended up damaging us both in irreparable ways. But it wasn't always like this.

My earliest memories of Momma are my fondest. She sang like a princess from an epic animated film. Her smile was like the brightest of sun-shiny days. Her touch was soothing and comforted the weariest of souls. Her conversations were enlightening and encouraging. She was a ball of energy. Furthermore, Momma was a Bible scholar who loved to read and write.

Brenda Joyce Hickman was a force to be reckoned with on absolutely every level: Pretty, personable, athletic, talented, confident, courageous, and brilliant. The seventh child of thirteen, she was the life of every party and the voice for all the voiceless. She was also the queen of reinvention—over the years, she evolved from housewife to food service professional, licensed cosmetologist to ultimately a nationally rated registered nurse. She was a tough act to follow.

My mother's death marked the end of one era and the beginning of another: Her story was written and her children's, without her now, is being written. Momma is no longer bound by time. She has entered eternity. We remain. Life without Momma mimics a limbo as we struggle to dance in the rain. We lean backward and get low but push forward with all our might to pass the bar with flying colors. It's lonely, but the music plays on. So, we dance. Momma loved to dance. She passed that love onto me and I now dance in her stead.

Upon her death, my siblings and I found stacks of journals. Each held a different part of my mother's story. All told of the internal struggles she battled, the joy she experienced, the doubts she developed, the celebrations, the fears, the laughter, the regrets, the tears, the unshakable faith, the disappointments, and the demise of a brilliant mind. As we read some of her private thoughts, we began to develop a better understanding of Momma. We wept, laughed, and were reintroduced to Momma, unfiltered, honest, and transparent in her own words.

The most precious gift Momma gave us was a beautiful introduction to Jesus Christ. She encouraged us to know Him for ourselves and taught us how to read the Word of God. Though eighteen years and one day was actually not *all* that separated Momma and me, she privately suffered an unbearable hurt that only God could heal. It was ever present, but so was her faith and hope in God. She poured into me during my lowest low, offered loving support to the many men and women who relied on her wisdom and wit, handled her sons and daughters-in-law with care, and showed unconditional love for her grandchildren.

I will forever love her because she was my mother. I will always respect her as my sister because we shared similar struggles and offenses at the hands of men. I will continue to embrace her as my friend because I could always count on her to tell me the whole unadulterated truth. She was a blessing to my life. I am her legacy and she is my legend. Because of her, I am able to soar past the pain and roar using my unique voice along the way.

As you continue to explore the pages of this book, you will discover things about yourself that have been masked for far too long. Have you ever been in a barren place? Do you live your life in fear? Have you ever considered suicide? Are you the quintessential people-pleaser? Do you feel invisible? Has divorce ruined your well-planned life? Is your joy suppressed by secrecy? You are not alone. These topics and many more will be addressed in the following pages.

Take inventory. Take notes. Take control. Get in position to grow in this space with us. Prepare to SOAR and ROAR as we invite you to become part of this sisterhood of common ground. Learn each of our SOARROARity™ rules and be inspired to develop your own.

My dear reader, my SOARROAR: I thought of you today. I saw you soaring throughout life with the confidence of a majestic hawk. I imagined you discovering all that you were created to be and it made me smile. I envisioned you accepting your reflection in the mirror and all its bountiful beauty. You embraced your place in the world and encouraged others to do the same.

You are incredible! You are intelligent! You make sound choices and welcome the wisdom of the elders. You are open to the many possibilities afforded to you to shift every environment for the better through your unique gifts and talents. You are making a difference in every life you encounter. You are an overcomer of many obstacles. You are a natural born problem solver. You are a descendant of royalty and you wear your crown well. You are the hope of many generations.

Your confidence is key to maintaining your momentum. Your faith is key to gaining clarity, establishing focus, and executing the proper action steps leading to your best self. Your gratitude is key to staying grounded and humble. Your resilience is key to moving forward after the distractions of adversity.

You are brilliant! You are innovative! You have the ability to create what has yet to be created. You have answers to the questions that have yet to be asked. You are a trendsetter, a go-getter, a heavy hitter, and a guaranteed winner! You add value to every relationship. You are an asset to your community. You are necessary.

I stand in agreement with you that your light will shine brightly. I decree and declare that your thoughts, words, and actions will align with your true purpose and calling. I believe with and for you that your living shall not be in vain. Yes, you will encounter difficulty, but you shall rise above it all. You will live to tell of a victorious comeback. Someone may break your heart but still the heart heals, and scars reveal the times you gave yourself permission to be vulnerable. If fear creeps in, stand against it with all your might. Ask for help; that's what sister friends are for, and none can do it all alone. So, surround yourself with those who mean you the best.

Laugh often. Dance. Hydrate. Cry both sad and happy tears. Love yourself and others unconditionally. Forgive yourself and others, but hold them accountable for their actions and be accountable for your actions. You will become more than you anticipated, even surpassing your biggest dreams! Own your prerogative to reinvent yourself when necessary. Teach the world how to treat you by treating yourself with the utmost love and respect, and do not be offended by what God is going to allow.

My SOARROARity™ Rules

Show up: You must be present. Do not live a passive life. Get in the game and run it by showing up first and on time, consistently.

Own up: You are not perfect. Be willing to own your imperfections and work on improving daily.

Act up: Positive, purposeful, centered, well thought-out, and calculated action will impact your life in the most beautiful way. Make a plan and execute without delay.

Rise-up: Consistently grow your elevation, increase the altitude of your attitude, and become a better version of yourself over time.

Resilience: Work on building your bounce-back muscle. We all fall down and sometimes we get knocked down. But you do not have to stay down—stand. Never allow your muscles to atrophy. Use them to capacity and beyond.

Optimism: Positivity goes a long way, taking you from hopelessness to hopefulness, but negativity depletes your soul. Focus on the brighter side of every situation. If none can be found, create it.

Accountability: Hold yourself and others accountable. Do your part. Contribute to improvement and accept nothing less than your best efforts.

Restored: Be restored by lending to the restoration of others. When you give of yourself, you grow out of self. The best return happens when you sow where you would like to grow.

SOAR~ROAR Reflection

1. What's the best advice someone has ever given to you?

2. List the results of taking that advice.

3. Who are the mentors or mothers in your life who pour the best wisdom into your cup when it is empty?

4. How are you now pouring into others what was poured into you?

5. List the generational dysfunctions that you are battling today.

6. What did you learn about yourself today?

7. Write an eight-sentence love letter to the one who has encouraged the most growth in you.

8. If the recipient of the letter is still living, mail it to them. If they are deceased, share it with a friend and celebrate the mentor.

DEANNA CUMMINGS

NO LONGER CAPTIVE
Freedom by Choice

Shackled by sin, shackled by men, shackled by the enemy that was hiding within me.

To lie to oneself is to hide from oneself. However, as my grandmother used to say, "The truth always comes to the light." But just because you bury something doesn't mean it's dead.

As a child, I became a master mortician of burying things, or so I thought. Those "things" didn't stay buried for long. In truth, I was laying the foundation for a prison in my mind, allowing myself to be shackled by untold truths.

Some of you may remember playing make believe as a child. I remember playing the game of forget. The premise of the game is to make yourself forget the things you don't want to remember. For instance, forget the inappropriate and uninvited abuse I suffered as a child. Forget being ripped from my home, my comfort zone, and finding myself in a sea of people who looked nothing like me but mostly like my mother (I say mostly because my younger brother and I are the result of an interracial marriage, which was still not acceptable by the masses back in the early 1970s).

I was born in Oakland, California, and raised primarily within my African American culture. So, when my Caucasian mother moved my brother and me away from what was familiar to us into a world of unfamiliarity, it was extremely difficult to adjust. Can you say culture shock? This new place, Gresham, Oregon, that I was forced to call home didn't look or feel anything like the home I'd grown accustomed to during the first five years of my life. I remember being afraid of the unknown, extremely sad, and withdrawn. I kept thinking, any day now, my dad is going to come for us and take us back home where we belong. But no such luck. Our dad would briefly come to town and visit from time to time, and my brother and I would get an opportunity to visit our family in California during the summer, but that was it. I remember never wanting to return to Oregon at the end of summer break; I dreaded the return every time.

Thankfully, my mother soon found the Sharon Seventh Day Adventist Church in Portland with people who not only looked like my brother and me, but were warm and welcoming as well. It didn't take long for this to become our new church home. It was here that the foundation was laid for my absolute love for my Lord and Savior Jesus Christ. This church holds so many wonderful memories for me, including meeting my first BFF and getting to know her family who became my extended family and a safe haven from the abuse I would shortly endure thereafter. The two of us shared the amazing experience of being baptized together, learning to worship in spirit and in truth, and hungering for the word of God. I am eternally grateful for my mother being instrumental in laying my spiritual foundation in Christ, which has been critical to my survival and I'm still building upon today. By far, that has been the greatest gift my mom ever gave me.

Prior to our move to Oregon, I attended public school. But now, I was enrolled at a private Christian school where I stood out as only one of six minorities in a school population that spanned grades one through twelve. Imagine my surprise when one day at school, where I was supposed to be in a structured and safe learning environment, a classmate verbally assaulted me by spewing venom so foul and vile I dare not repeat it. I'm sure you can imagine what was said. It wasn't the first time such words were spoken and, sadly, it would not be the last. I know there have been far greater travesties, but in that moment, I felt isolated and set apart from the other children. At a time when I was hoping to make new friends and somehow try to make the best out of this relocation, my self-confidence took another blow.

Here I was, this displaced little girl from California who, I thought, wasn't supposed to be in Oregon in the first place. I should've been back in California with my dad and the rest of my family. Instead, I was in this new place, suffering from the heaviness of Triple A: Abuse, alienation, and abandonment. I was dealing with abuse at the hands of family members, alienation based on the color of my skin, and feelings of abandonment by my father and everything familiar to me. The weight of it all was extremely heavy for my young shoulders to bear, though somehow, I did.

Just when I was beginning to think that this new place wasn't so bad after all, "it" began again. "It" being the word I'm choosing to describe the abuse I suffered at the hands of family members yet *again*. Initially, my instincts said, "Hold up. Aren't you supposed to love and protect me?" But instead, I allowed the additional weight of heaviness to silence me once more.

I found myself depositing more secrets into my memory bank. Oh, how I wished I could close the account and make no withdrawals at all; simply close it and be done, but that was not the case. You can't close an account without notifying someone, and I didn't feel like telling anyone was an option for me. Fear had a tight grip on my body and a muzzle over my mouth, so I would incur mounting fees based on the number of secret deposits made into my memory bank. This was due solely to the account's inability to store such a mass volume of secrets. As a result, there was spillage that ran over into other areas of my life.

I began to condition my mind, soul and body to carry the weight of secrecy. "It," though just a two-letter word, became a huge and unbearable weight over time that caused a substantial negative impact and pulled me deeper into the secret society of captivity. Fear gripped me and secrets ripped me—but I would soon learn that I had been shackled since I was even younger.

After a year or so passed, I realized this relocation wasn't merely a brief interruption of the life I once knew in California—my mother, brother, and I were going to be here for a while. Oregon was a place we stayed unaccompanied, aside from my dad's occasional visits. I was a daddy's girl so the void of his everyday absence was quite painful to bear. I also believed deep down that if my daddy were there with us he'd be able to protect me from the Triple A. He was everything to me and his absence left me feeling empty and alone. I didn't feel safe sharing my secrets with anyone.

Then one day, out of the blue and almost five years after the separation, my parents announced that they were getting back together. This was music to my ears like the Peaches and Herb 1978 album song, "Reunited." And yes, it felt so good! This meant we'd be a family again. Most importantly, we'd move back to California, the place I always considered home. This knowledge empowered me and allowed me to stand up to my adversary in a way that caused a cease-fire in his attacks against me. I know in my heart of hearts that it was God freeing me from fear that had forced my compliance. There's something to be said for individually standing up in my God-given authority and declaring, "No more!" No more would he violate me. No more would I buckle and cower in fear. No more would I allow him to control me. No more would I be a prisoner to his perversion. I believe this was one of my early attempts at soaring above my circumstances, standing up for myself, and taking back my God-given authority.

It was during my teenage years that I re-discovered the secrets I had buried some time ago. To my dismay, they were very much alive and had obviously caused a devastating impact on my self-confidence, which had begun welcoming the attention of young men and sexual promiscuity as I looked for love in all the wrong places. I wish I could have asked for help, owned my truth, and gotten the healing I so desperately needed. Sure, on the outside looking in, my family was back together and I was no longer captive to abuse. So life was great, right? Wrong!

I began to hurt myself through eating my feelings, while the pain ate away at me. Good food has been comforting to me as far back as I can remember. Whether my mood was happy, mad, or sad, food was somewhere in the equation and, honestly, it still is. This also affected my self-worth, as my weight issues yo-yo-ed up and down. Why couldn't I be skinny? Why was my butt so big? Why was my hair so thick? Nothing about me looked bi-racial, but I was and am. I was even asked a time or two if I had been adopted until they'd see my mom and make out the resemblances for themselves. I didn't even have the so-called "pretty hair" that most mixed children were blessed to have. I think I was most upset about not having that trait, especially since I loved swimming and my hair was not swim-friendly

Yes, I became good at tearing myself down. And that self-hatred combined with the built-up secrecy threatened to rob me of my God-given destiny. Granted, I was so happy to be reunited as a family and have my daddy back as a permanent fixture in my life. He was an amazing father who loved us and provided well for our family; at one time, he was working three jobs to afford our family's needs as well as our wants. But I was still broken and needed repair.

Fast forward to me giving birth to my first son at the youthful age of twenty years old. At the time, I was enrolled at Sacramento State University by way of an academic scholarship, majoring in criminal justice. This was in no way a good time to tell my parents that their eldest child, the one they held to high standards and placed their hopes in, had derailed from the track of success by getting pregnant. Eventually, I would have to withdraw from school.

I can vividly recall my mother in the kitchen, chopping vegetables on the cutting board, preparing our weeknight dinner as I spilled my guts about the pregnancy. I remember her stopping mid-chop and the look of disappointment fall on her face. I felt like I failed her. My tear-stained face was swollen and my breathing uncontrolled as my father came through the door from work. He saw me in what had to appear to him as utter despair and asked me what was wrong. I was choked up with agonizing fear for what I knew would be the same look of disappointment in his face. I could barely speak the words, but I eventually did in between hyperventilating: "I'm pregnant."

I tried desperately to brace myself for my dad's reaction, though I didn't think that was actually possible. However, in that moment, I didn't see rage or disappointment on his face. My dad offered me grace! He gave me the gift of sweet, amazing grace in that moment of terror. His response was, "Stop crying, Dee. Dry your eyes. There's nothing you can do about it now." He even went as far as to get tissues from the bathroom and hand them to me so that I could clean my snotty face. This was not the response I anticipated at all, but I was so very thankful just the same. After the initial shock wore off, my mother came around and, before you knew it, we were planning a baby shower and looking forward to the arrival of my son, DeAndre.

I went on to marry his father despite all the red flags. Aren't we good at ignoring the signs and then wondering, "How'd I get here?" Well, I'm guilty as charged, guilty of lending a blind eye despite having 20/20 vision. Nevertheless, three sons, DeAndre, Brandon, and Aaron, were born to us during our fifteen years of living together as husband and wife.

My marriage and my children were everything to me. I promise you, I did everything within my power to make it work. I prayed and even continued to ignore the signs of repeated infidelity. I internalized my husband's faults as my own. I even relocated to another state in an attempt to keep our family together. I left behind a career with a company rated in the top fifty companies to work for, where I was well compensated and on the fast track for advancement. After reaching the point of no return, I decided it was time for another burial, this time for my marriage. But this burial, I would not mourn alone and the impact would be quite costly to everyone involved, especially my sons, my gifts from God.

When I made up my mind to separate and later file for divorce from my husband, the process would prove to be one of the toughest but most necessary decisions I ever made. Over time, I learned to disguise the pain and live in a façade. Looking back now, I find it odd. Odd that no one else could see the chains that held me in captivity. I wanted so badly to be freed from both past and present pains that threatened to overtake me. It was then that I decided to call upon His name, the name of Jesus. And He heard my cry.

Unbeknownst to me and my broken vision, not only had He heard me, but He cared for me. Yes, God cared in all my brokenness and was willing to mend the broken pieces of my life and restore me in order to deliver me from the weight of secrecy, pain, and shame. But I was required to forgive, and forgive I did. I no longer harbor anger, resentment, or bitterness towards those who abused or misused me. Rather, I choose to lay them at the cross and trust God to heal, deliver, and set them free from their own captivity.

Following this life-altering decision, I began to seek God like never before. On my journey of rediscovering my Lord and Savior in a more intimate way, I also discovered who He created me to be. I realized then that I was never intended to be held hostage by the heaviness of secrecy or bound by the chains of self-destruction. Not only had I been carrying the weight of my own heaviness, but I had also been carrying the weight of those I loved. No longer! My season of captivity was over—I was being released and no longer confined by pains designed to keep me entrapped. I became focused on what lie ahead of me and chose to let go of everything else.

I no longer felt entangled; instead, I was liberated and free. God's word tells us in John 8:36 (KJV), "If the Son therefore shall make you free, you shall be free indeed." The closer I drew to God, the better my understanding became of who He is and who He says I am. I am now able to stand firmly on the promises of God, and I'd like to share a few of my favorite passages:

- [The righteous] cry, and the LORD heareth, and delivereth them out of all their troubles (Psalms 34:17 (KJV)).

- Stand fast therefore in the liberty wherewith Christ hath made us free, and be not entangled again with the yoke of bondage (Galatians 5:1 (KJV)).

- But if ye forgive not men their trespasses, neither will your Father forgive your trespasses (Matthew 6:15 (KJV)).

- If we confess our sins, he is faithful and just to forgive us [our] sins, and to cleanse us from all unrighteousness (1 John 1:9).

- Come unto me, all [ye] that labor and are heavy laden, and I will give you rest (Matthew 11:28 (KJV)).

- I can do all things through Christ, which strengtheneth me (Philippians 4:13 (KJV)).

- He healeth the broken in heart, and bindeth up their wounds (Psalms 147:3 (KJV)).

- But they that wait upon the LORD shall renew [their] strength; they shall mount up with wings as eagles; they shall run, and not be weary; [and] they shall walk, and not faint (Isaiah 40:31 (KJV)).

Those power-packed promises are life-changing if you allow them to be. I haven't even put a dent in all that I know God has pre-destined for me to accomplish, but I'm well on my way because of His leading and my submission to His will for my life. Obedience is fundamental to achieving your God-given destiny, which you can ACCESS by:

- **A**ccepting whose you are
- **C**larifying your purpose
- **C**anceling out the
- **E**nemy's untruths in order to
- **S**ubmit to the will of God and
- **S**oar

Close your eyes and imagine God standing with His arms outstretched, holding your personalized ACCESS card to freedom in His hand. Do you want ACCESS? The journey isn't easy, but it's necessary. To soar is to be free; there's freedom in your soar!

But before you spread your wings, I'd like to share a few more things. The following are my rules to SOAR and ROAR. Each rule will give you some tools to ensure your release from captivity. Lastly, I'd like to leave you with some thought-provoking questions of self-assessment to begin the necessary shift out of captivity into the promised land of freedom to soar.

My SOARROARity™ Rules

Surrender to God's perfect will so you can

Overcome your past by

Acknowledging your truths and

Remaining committed to God's design.

Resist the heaviness of various

Oppressions that seek to entangle you,

And war in the spirit through prayer and supplication with thanksgiving.

Reclaim your freedom to soar.

SOAR~ROAR Reflection

1. Are you keeping secrets you're too ashamed to share?
2. Do you blame yourself for things that were out of your control?
3. Have you forgiven the perpetrator of your pain?
4. Are you currently walking in your truth?
5. Do you know Jesus the Son of God?
6. Are you aware of the power and authority you possess on the inside?
7. What steps are you willing to take to ensure freedom from your past?
8. Are you ready to soar?

RONDA BAILEY

FROM A SHAMEFUL PAST TO A VICTORIOUS DESTINY

Overcoming your Past and Boldly Stepping into Your Purpose

> "I prayed to the Lord, and he answered me. He freed me from all my fears. Those who look to him for help will be radiant with joy; no shadow of shame will darken their faces."
>
> —*Psalm 34:4-5*

As a Christ follower, wife, mother, and entrepreneur, I have journeyed through deep pain, feelings of inadequacy, and shame. In every season of life, I have encountered many other women who have had and currently have the same struggles. Women just like me who don't understand their purpose, beauty, power, or worth. Most trade the truth about their struggles for worldly acceptance. Although our past pains and current obstacles to living in true freedom may vary, we often find commonality in living in facades, hiding from ourselves, and disguising our scars. Many fall into the trap of believing that their past defines them, that what happened to them dictates who they are and who they have the potential to be.

I share my story of coming from a point of pain, guilt, shame, and regret to reaching a state of true freedom and becoming the author of my own destiny. My story will inspire you to not only accept your past and truths, but to have the audacity to be truly victorious despite them.

It was afterschool and I was rushing to finish my chores before the four o'clock showing of *The Oprah Winfrey Show*. I folded the towels, socks, and underwear as quickly as I could; then practically unfolding my work, I haphazardly tossed them into their assigned drawers.

"Done!" A quick glance at the clock radio in my parent's bedroom showed 4:02. I made a mad dash to the living room where the opening song and credits had already passed and Oprah was bringing out her first panel of guests. I was so excited to see what this woman, whom I admired greatly, would share today. Zoning into the television, I barely noticed my father and mother both step into the living room. My father took his usual spot on his recliner, my mother on the sofa. I was already seated on the floor. As I leaned in to absorb today's show, the conversation on the screen began to give me feelings of what I would later understand to be anxiety. The panel of guests on Oprah's show that day were psychologists, experts, and adult survivors of childhood sexual abuse.

Suddenly, I wished that somehow, someway, the floor would just open up and swallow me whole. I did my best to act normal, to not let my exasperation show. I cautiously looked out of the corner of my eyes to see if my parents were showing any reaction to the show's topic. None. Zilch. Poker faces. Completely expressionless. I bit my trembling lip to command it to be still and rapidly blinked back the tears I could feel forming.

How could they? How could they sit there emotionless while this panel discussed the damage done to these women? How could my mother watch this show knowing the history of complaints and accusations against my father? How could my father sit there completely unbothered by the noted, ongoing negative impact an abuser has on his or her victim?

I was twelve years old at the time, and the abuse had been going on at least since I was seven. My father, who had been sexually abusing me for almost five years at this point, showed no emotional response to Oprah's show topic, as if the panel wasn't speaking directly to my pain. My abuse. My subsequent struggles. My life.

A commercial came on and the volume was ten times louder than the show. I started to refocus. There was no way I was going to get up and leave the room even amidst my anxiety. I felt paralyzed with the task of finishing the show, of listening in for nuggets of information that could be of help to me. I watched, listened, and endured the remaining forty-five minutes. Not once did I move from my spot or even turn my head to make eye contact with either of my parents to see their lack of emotion or response to the show. I was so deep in my own thoughts that I only captured snippets of the content. Unfortunately, those pieces did not include any "victories" from the horrific experiences. But what I did glean from the show was a connection between sexual abuse victims and promiscuity, victims and abusive behavior, victims and drug addictions, victims and mental health issues. Victims continuing to be victims.

The panel seemed to agree: What else could you expect from victims of childhood sexual abuse? Damaged goods forever. Fragility. Instability. Years and years of therapy. "No thanks," I thought. Not for me. I was already tired of being a victim silently; it seemed that, if I were to tell someone, I'd be further treated as a victim for the rest of my life. I knew right then that I would have to continue to keep my secret locked away. I did not want to be seen as a victim—I would allow no one to assume that. Because of what had happened and was continuing to happen to me, my destiny would be as painful as my past.

I made a pact with myself to take my secret to my grave. Hiding my pain seemed easier than dealing with the label of "victim." In my young pre-adolescent mind, I thought my decision to cover up the abuse and shameful family secret would be the best way to protect myself. I had always been quiet anyway because my father made it clear that if anyone found out, it would be me who would be taken away from our family and placed with strangers who may not love me at all, or even feed me for that matter. I would end up starving in a basement if I said anything.

I began junior high school, understanding more and more about how people perceive others and how we make judgments based on current and/or past circumstances. Suddenly, outward appearances mattered so much more than they had before. I had always felt a little different and less included than some of my friends throughout elementary school and I very much desired to be popular in junior high. I learned what "normal" families did together. I made new friends. I started to be careful about how much I shared about my home life. I was excelling in my academics, extra-curricular activities, and church commitments. I was busy achieving and building up the "image" I thought was necessary for me to be accepted and included. As a seventh grader, I was developing my master plan to not appear like a victim.

I hoped that my academic achievements would one day be my ticket away from the abusive home I grew up in. I kept myself as busy as possible to spend minimal time at home, and became an obsessive reader otherwise. Often, after another violation by my father, I would privately sulk for a couple days, envying many of my friends who truly adored their fathers. Why couldn't I have a father who would love me the way a father should? Sometimes, I even thought I would be better off if I were like some of my other friends, who had no fathers in their lives. I resolved to keep my mouth shut and my grades up—that would be my way out eventually.

Throughout the next few years until I graduated, I became an expert about concealing the shameful parts of my family's life. I avoided sharing personal details as to deter follow-up questions and would even revise current circumstances into a lie that would be better received. The thought of being labeled as "damaged goods" was still too much for me to bear. I continued to build my fake exterior and it was working. No one knew what I was going through at home, even my closest friends.

I felt as though I finally got my break when one of my top college choices, located out of state, awarded me with a sizable scholarship. I can still remember cutting the tiny notice out of our local paper. Freedom from this life would be soon, I believed. But my life at that college never happened. I had even visited the school, met some of my professors, had a roommate assignment, and even completed my summer reading assignment when I realized I would not be going. My mother told me that we just couldn't afford to pay the additional tuition and I would need to go elsewhere. We had always grown up without much and I figured that this was yet another thing we couldn't afford. I ended up enrolling at the local university instead for that fall.

I tried to tell myself that this would work out great too; after all, I had a couple friends attending the same university. I moved out of my parents' home the summer after high school graduation. The struggle of suppressing my truth became increasingly taxing over the next few years. I started to party a lot, my grades slipped, and I was in danger of losing my scholarship. Eventually, I decided to move away from the town I had grown up in. I got a place of my own, found a decent job, and promised myself I would enroll in another local college after I was settled. I figured going back to school could wait a little; after all, I was making good money and taking care of myself without the help of anyone else, all at nineteen. I knew of a lot of people who went back to school as adults, so I figured I could do the same.

My lifestyle, at times, was reckless. Party after party, spending every dime of my paycheck every week, no additional plans for my future except for the "One day, I'll go back to school." Occasionally, I would get a warning of the internal damage I was causing myself. Twice I reached out to a stranger on a crisis hotline just to cry out, just to tell someone of my secret past that was beginning to torment me more. Working, partying, and spending money were my distractions now, my escape.

Within a few months of moving to the city, I met a guy who I really liked, who I would fall in love with and later marry. As we dated and he got to know me, I was cautious about revealing my past—I mean, who wants to date a girl with so much baggage? I continued with my fake history. Four and a half years later, we married. I was miserable planning my wedding because I knew I didn't have the courage to tell the truth about my family. I'd always wanted a traditional church wedding in a white dress with bridesmaids, flower girls, the whole nine yards. I chose to have my father walk me down the aisle. It pains me even to this day to view the photos from our wedding. I was so ashamed of the truth that I was willing to tarnish my own wedding experience and memories just to continue to paint a picture of normalcy. So ashamed. I continued to live with my altered reality and became stuck. I had lied and been silent for so long, if I were to say something now, would anyone even believe me?

One Saturday morning, almost a year into our marriage, I knew I couldn't continue on any longer. My husband and I were enjoying coffee on the porch, talking about the right time to have a child together, and I knew that I couldn't start the next chapter of my life without owning up to the fictitious story my life had become. I told him everything. Sharing my truth with someone who deeply loved me was the hardest and greatest thing I've ever done for myself. But my anxiety of telling the truth about my past was quickly tamed by my husband's heartfelt and emotional response. His immediate hug and words of reassurance gave me life and the love I needed to move forward and begin healing. In that moment I knew I no longer had to continue this journey alone.

I started seeing a counselor for the first time. Months of therapy and practical exercises helped me to release pain, shame, and insecurities that had built up over time from years of abuse and cover-up. Although the sessions were sometimes painful, all those secrets spilled out of my soul. I learned about boundaries and how I had been living my life without them. I was grateful for the breakthrough.

Although counseling sessions had given me some tangible ways to recover from my past abuse and to set up appropriate boundaries in my life, I still didn't feel like I was truly a conqueror of my own circumstances. I still struggled with feelings of inadequacy and didn't believe that I would be able to really live a life of freedom. As I began to attend church again, I could feel a sense of belonging and a true tugging at my heart. I started to reconnect with God.

What I didn't realize at first is that God was already present and ready to help lift me out of my despair, I just needed to call out to Him. As I continued to attend church each Sunday, I started to make small, but significant changes in my habits. I read short passages out of the Bible, I followed devotionals, and I started praying daily. I wrote down scriptures that spoke to me about God's true promises. I realized that God never promised Christians that we wouldn't go through hard times, but that He would use those difficulties to strengthen and mold us.

I started to understand the real power of words and thoughts, and that the enemy tries to attack you directly in your mind through the way you view yourself and your circumstances. I grew my relationship deeper with God, trying to make sense of it all. As I stretched in my faith and served more in my church, I was approached about coming on-board to work in the church I was growing to love. I knew that their work was changing lives—they had certainly made an impact on mine and my family's—so I jumped at the opportunity.

Working full-time in ministry was unlike anything I had ever experienced before—it was so rewarding, but draining at the same time. I was the children's ministry director after only being on staff for a short time. I found that many of the volunteers and staff I worked with were also struggling with different challenges from their past or current circumstances. I could offer guidance and encouragement, but inside, I still felt like a fraud. Others viewed me as a spiritual leader, someone who was living life in purpose, but I wasn't sure if that truly described me. I realized then that I could not fully step into my God-given purpose until I walked with true authenticity.

I began to pray to God about how and when to share my testimony. He revealed to me the step that I would need to take to really recover and begin a new life of freedom in Him: Forgive. At the time, forgiveness wasn't something that I felt I could truly offer to my abuser or to the adults in my family who turned a blind eye. I always had a misconception that forgiveness meant that I would have to accept the offenders back into my life.

One day at church, there was a message on forgiveness. I had heard many messages and read several devotions about forgiveness, but would always counter with, "But what I went through *really* is unforgiveable." This message was different: It pointed out that we didn't have to have a relationship with someone as proof of forgiveness and that forgiveness is about *me*, not my abuser. That forgiveness would allow *me* to come out from under my pain and give to God my deepest hurts. That forgiveness for *me* meant no longer wishing that the past hadn't happened. It meant that *I* would no longer have to wish for revenge on my abuser. It didn't mean that I had to love my father the way one should love his or her parents, but it did mean that I had to recognize that he was also a child of God and that God loves all His children. His salvation through Christ Jesus should be something that I prayed for fervently.

It wasn't easy to turn the corner of forgiveness. I had to faith it until I made it. The more I understood God's love, mercy, and forgiveness, the closer I became to my true freedom. To this day, I must continue to *choose* forgiveness. It is not a one-time event. If I see my father or hear mention of him, my feelings of hurt from my past start to rise to the surface, and time after time, I have had to actively choose the action of forgiveness. I must continue to stand firm in the understanding of my worth through my Heavenly Father.

Throughout the next several years, I continued to heal from my past, claimed my identity in Christ, and became bolder about sharing my testimony in hopes of helping others. I unlocked some key principles in recovering from a point of shame to a mindset of abundance and resiliency.

My SOARROARity™ Rules

Seek to understand your worth and who you are designed to be through the eyes of God. True freedom comes when we begin to view ourselves the way our Father sees us. I understand that it's not easy: In the early days of my journey, I couldn't trust that our Father in Heaven really had me in His hands. My earthly father had failed so miserably to provide a safe place or home of trust that I found it challenging at first to entirely put my trust in my Heavenly Father alone.

> "I will praise You, for I am fearfully and wonderfully made; Marvelous are Your works, and that my soul knows very well."
>
> —*Psalm 139:14*

> "For I know the plans I have for you," declares the Lord, "plans to prosper you and not to harm you, plans to give you hope and a future."
>
> —*Jeremiah 29:11*

Open your heart to forgiveness. Continue daily to choose to forgive—this must be an intentional action because you will not *feel* like you want to forgive. Concentrate on what forgiveness means for you and your circumstances. Forgiveness doesn't always mean that you must continue to have a relationship with the one you forgive. Being able to choose forgiveness opens up the relationship between you and God, which allows true freedom.

Even as a survivor I had to choose to forgive myself. I realized I was resentful towards myself for choosing to cover up the truth and prolonging my pain and agony for so many years.

> "But I say to you, love your enemies, bless those who curse you, do good to those who hate you, and pray for those who spitefully use you and persecute you."
>
> —*Matthew 5:44*

> "Let all bitterness, wrath, anger, clamor, and evil speaking be put away from you, with all malice. And be kind to one another, tenderhearted, forgiving one another, even as God in Christ forgave you."
>
> —*Ephesians 4:31-32*

Accept your past as your past. You are not what happened to you, and you are not defined by your mistakes. Stop wasting energy and power on wishing away the events that have shaped you into who you are today. God can and will use everything for your good, but you need to accept your past and allow Him to work you through it. Your testimony will help you and others.

> "You intended to harm me, but God intended it all for good. He brought me to this position so I could save the lives of many people."
>
> —*Genesis 50:20*

Reach out for additional support, if needed. This could be in the form of therapy, a counselor, books and workbooks, support groups, prayer groups, and even community groups. It's important that you have a network of support, especially while you are progressing through and past your pain.

Rejoice in the power that God has given you to live a life of freedom and abundance. Victims of abuse and those stuck in a pattern of shame feel powerless because they don't believe that they have control over their own lives. Reclaim that power by courageously redefining yourself through the eyes of God, despite your circumstances, so that you may tap into the power that God has already place inside you.

> "Now all glory to God, who is able, through his mighty power at work within us, to accomplish infinitely more than we might ask or think."
>
> —*Ephesians 3:20*

Own your thoughts. Protect your mind continuously. Your thoughts and words determine who you are, so recognize your internal voice and change the script if necessary.

> "And now, dear brothers and sisters, one final thing. Fix your thoughts on what is true, and honorable, and right, and pure, and lovely, admirable. Think about things that are excellent and worthy of praise. Keep putting into practice all you learned and received from me - everything you heard from me and saw me doing. Then the God of peace will be with you."
>
> —*Philippians 4:8-9*

Audaciously step out and allow yourself the gift of a new beginning. Be assured in your greatness, for you are the child of the one true King, and cling to that identity, not the one the world or your abuser may have slapped on you. Live in that greatness despite your past.

> "But forget all that- it is nothing compared to what I am going to do. For I am about to do something new. See, I have already begun! Do you not see it? I will make a pathway through the wilderness. I will create rivers in the dry wasteland."
>
> —*Isaiah 43:18-19*

Receive the blessings in your life with the understanding that you are deserving and worthy in the eyes of your Heavenly Father.

> "Whatever is good and perfect is a gift coming down to us from God our Father, who created all the lights in the heavens. He never changes or casts a shifting shadow."
>
> —*James 1:17*

Application of these rules will be the key to successfully taking back your power and truly creating a life of love, acceptance, abundance, and most of all, freedom. It is impossible to heal from that which is hidden. My life has changed in immeasurable ways because of this journey. I *know* that I am the daughter of the King of kings and I am loved. I have a strong, incredible marriage of fifteen years, I have amazing daughters, and I am a successful business owner and entrepreneur. I am a published author, speaker, and giver of life! I am worthy, I am more than enough, I am a conqueror, and I am victorious! I am resilient in the face of adversity. I am boldly stepping out in faith to take my story to the world with the expectation that God will use it for good. I have the audacity and the courage to step up, speak out, and change the world, despite those who tried to harm and silence me.

SOAR~ROAR Reflection

1. In what areas have you been harmed?

2. Are there some situations that silenced your most authentic voice? List them.

3. What affirmations will you declare for yourself today?

4. List some examples of your strength in action.

5. Describe how you plan to step out on faith from this day forward.

6. Speak affirming statements several times throughout each day.

7. Compile a list of those who will support you in your healing from the past.

JOCELYN L. WALLACE

THE MIDDLE PASSAGE OF MY NAME
What's Love Got to Do With It?

Want to know a secret? Do you want to know *my* secret? It's something that everyone seeks but is often not found. It's often abused, misused, and second-guessed. It's the only real thing that we as a human race can rely on. It's what conditioned me.

I am Jocelyn "Love" Wallace. Though the name Jocelyn and Wallace are common, I'd like to think my name is special as I hope you think yours is too. My name is special because of its unique identifier: My middle name is Love. I love Love because it is so powerful. It's powerful when said. It's powerful when written. It's powerful when drawn and it's even more powerful when it's shown. Love groomed me. Love nurtured me. Love saved me. Love is the secret ingredient to life's recipe.

A common Bible verse was referenced in my family during many occasions so that I was always reminded of the power of love:

> "Charity suffereth long, and is kind; charity envieth not; charity vaunteth not itself, is not puffed up, Doth not behave itself unseemly, seeketh not her own, is not easily provoked, thinketh no evil; Rejoiceth not in iniquity, but rejoiceth in the truth; Beareth all things, believeth all things, hopeth all things, endureth all things. Charity never faileth: but whether there be prophecies, they shall fail; whether there be tongues, they shall cease; whether there be knowledge, it shall vanish away" (1 Corinthians 13:4-8 KJV).

This verse was instrumental in the foundational blueprint of my life, though I didn't understand it's meaning until adulthood when I was able to apply it to my own life experiences. Since then, this verse has greatly influenced my successes and my disappointments.

Love is patient and Love is kind…

On Wednesday, July 30, I was born to David and Hope Wallace. My father was a soldier in the United States Air Force and later worked in law enforcement. My mother worked in the casino industry as well as in law enforcement. I have an older sister and her name is Crystal. Though small in size, we were a mighty family whose foundation was based on God's unconditional love and our love for each other.

During my formative years, there were moments that reminded me that I was loved. I was provided a house to build a home in, food to eat, clothes to wear, a sister to share experiences with, and parents who counseled, disciplined and mentored me. My parents were each other's pillars in the marriage, but they were also the pillars of my life since they were my first examples of love. From their love, I knew how to love. But I also learned that love doesn't always last.

At the age of five, my parents divorced and I didn't quite understand why. All I understood was that my parents were no longer living in the same household and I had to be transported weekly to either one of their homes in which my upbringing was different per household. My father's house was structured, given the military background. There were tons of rules and tasks and it was a given that we went to church every Sabbath no matter what. My father's love is what I like to call a firm love. However, my mother's house was more relaxed. There were rules but less structure and a "fend for yourself" parenting mentality. I identify my mother's love as free-spirited. Though no parenting method was better than the other, through each experience, I learned that there were different ways to love.

My family life started to shift when my father met another woman who he dated for a short period and then married. Our small family became blended. Surprisingly, we were not dysfunctional, but rather a real family working together towards the betterment of my sister's and my childhood.

One of the most memorable moments of my childhood is a true "there must be a God" situation. I was probably nine or ten years old. It was a sunny day in the summer months of Las Vegas. My mother, sister, and I were at a park, sitting at a picnic table to play games. I turned to my right and saw my dad's wife (my step-mom) approaching the table. Naturally, my reaction was to become defensive and protect my mother because there was no reason for my stepmom to be there. However, I was reminded of the one commonality both women in my life shared with each other: The children. Upon acknowledgment of one another, both of my mothers embraced with open arms and gave each other friendly greetings as if they had been friends for years! Though I was young, I couldn't help but feel awkward. Wouldn't you? How were my dad's second wife and his first wife getting along? Needless to say, we enjoyed ourselves at the park and all I could think was "Wow!"

We are loved. I am loved unconditionally despite my parent's separation. Society has a way of saying to us that co-parenting isn't possible, divorced homes are broken, and love is conditional. We can no longer limit ourselves to the small mindsets of others. It's imperative that we love one another past each other's faults. It was an "ah-ha" moment that showed me that no matter the circumstance, I can block out the negative noise, set aside differences, and do all things in love. Most importantly, I can shine on and allow no one to tell me what love is supposed to look or feel like.

> **Love does not envy. Love is not self-seeking.
> Love is not easily angered.
> Love keeps no record of wrongs…**

My family was getting along and I felt like I could conquer the world. I was full of love. I felt invincible until I had to attend middle school. Who would've thought that, by the age of thirteen, I would have experienced so many pressures of the world, resulting in low-self esteem, self-hatred, unworthiness, and defeat?

Now you know about my parent's divorce and the positive outcome in the context of parenting. However, I must also mention how the divorce affected me negatively. At a young age, I realized God was the author of my life and things that transpired had to be approved by Him personally. Therefore, I knew my parent's divorce wasn't a mistake, but it most certainly taught me a few things. It taught me that my parents' love for me is unconditional and that love can be available for family, friends, or significant others. But what about self-love?

My foundational make-up was always comprised of love and loving others but I didn't realize that also meant loving myself. In my formative years, I didn't worry about my weight, even though I was a big girl. I just understood that the body I had was the body God wanted me to be in. I looked just like my father who was a good-looking man, and he knew it, too! So, if he loved the way he looked, I must love the way I looked. Well, it wasn't until I was bullied in school that I realized that my body was a problem.

I was always pretty for a big girl. I was always the smart one. I was always the teacher's pet. I was always the goodie-two-shoes who didn't lie, cheat, steal, or harm others. If I knew I was my teacher's favorite student, Honey, I held that position with honor so I could learn as much as possible from that teacher. Was I wrong? I certainly didn't think so.

Growing up, I didn't have much compared to others but I worked with what I had. My family lived as humble as possible and I was not raised to glorify material possessions because all I needed was God, family, and an education. My parents clothed me with the basic wears. I had two pairs of shoes that I wore every school year and I rotated my outfits daily for school. I was teased for my weight, and also for my not-so-cute face, my hygiene, and the greatest of all time: Talking white. I never understood what that meant. I didn't use profanity and I spoke using complete sentences. To me that was the English language, but what did I know?

From the age of ten to thirteen, I took care of myself by waking up early, showering, getting dressed, styling my hair, and going to school. I lived in a single parent home and, often times, I was left alone. No disrespect to my mother because she had to work, but I had to learn to take care of myself the best way I knew how. I battled with depression because I started to believe I was ugly. I eventually smelled my body odor and felt even uglier to the point that I made up my mind: I didn't deserve to live. I was jealous of all the girls at school who had boyfriends or wore the latest and greatest outfits. I was angry at God for making me look this way. I was angry at my parents for not reminding me that I was enough. I was mad at my sister for not protecting me from my bullies. I was mad at myself for being me. Why me?

One Friday night, my mother left for work (she worked graveyard for the casino) and my sister was in her room asleep. It was around 11:00 PM and I was wide awake. I took out a piece of paper and I started writing a letter to God. I wrote a full page of questions to God. Why had He made me like this? Why did I look like this? Why couldn't I look like Ashley, Dominique, or Tori? What purpose was there for me to live? As I was writing, phrases kept repeating in my mind: "You are invisible, no one loves you, you are ugly, you smell, you are not enough, you don't deserve to live so you should just go now."

Time was drifting and, eventually, I finished writing the letter to God. Then I started to write a letter to my mother, my sister, and my father. After those were done, I nervously grabbed a sharp knife from the kitchen, went back to my room, and sat on the floor with my back against the wall. I cried and cried and cried. I started aiming the knife towards my arm and I dug as hard as I could into my veins, enough to start a cut. Though tiny, the cut was definitely a manifestation of the emotional pain I felt and it was overwhelming.

I started to bleed and immediately grabbed a towel and applied pressure. I remember crying so much that, upon my next effort to dig an even deeper cut, my eyes became heavy and I experienced an overpowering feeling of lethargy that made me go straight to sleep.

The next morning, I awoke upset because I was living another day. However, I had to move forward as if nothing ever happened. Being that it was a Saturday and a day of worship, I had to prepare for church. I was tired and still angry. At church, our pastor preached a sermon called "Why Not?" It was as if the pastor had been there with me Friday night, had read my letter to God and my family, and was now repeating every question I had asked God during his sermon. He said, "As Christians, we question God all the time and continuously ask Him, 'Why are we going through this and that? Why her? Why him? Why me?' God is saying 'Why not?'"

When I heard the pastor say "Why not?" I received immediate clarity. I realized that God chose me to go through this valley experience because He needed to remind me that I was strong and, through Him, all things are possible. He needed to remind me that I was more than enough and, as long as I continued to look to Him, He would always have my back!

God takes us through the valley so that we can be a vessel for Him, help others overcome their struggles, and remind them that we will eventually make it to the mountaintop.

Have you ever had a valley experience? Have you ever felt like giving up?

I assure you that God is truly in the blessing business and, like He saved me from defeat by way of suicide, He will save you. The moment we realize our lives aren't about us but about a greater need to serve others, the more we open ourselves to receive countless blessings. Be obedient to the Word of God and stand on His promises. God will not leave us or forsake us. He loves us in spite of our own missteps. He loves us unconditionally but we have to continue to lean on him.

Love bears all things. Love believes all things. Love hopes for and endures all things.

Let's recap. By the age of thirteen, I learned about unconditional love first from God then my parents. I also learned about loving others and loving myself. So, what else is there to learn about love? What about being *in* love? Yes…boys! You gotta' love them, right?

My first crush was in middle school and he was a star athlete, standing at 5'8 and *fine*! He was one of the most popular guys in school but what I liked about him the most was that he liked curvy girls. He liked curvy girls so much that, once all the curvy girls found out they were the flavor of the year, he dated all of them but me.

In high school, I liked a couple of guys. My first crush was just a physical attraction but I learned he had nothing to offer me but his cute, hazel eyes. However, my second crush was average and he loved the Lord. He lived close to my neighborhood, went to church faithfully, respected women, loved his family, and was saving himself for marriage—just like me.

I am still a virgin to this day! Remember when I mentioned that my father worked in law enforcement? Well, he worked with youth ages ten to seventeen years old, who were always getting into trouble. Some of the kids were gang bangers, prostitutes, and runaways, homeless or abandoned. Being that my father was overprotective, he oftentimes shared stories of the girls he mentored (I think it was a scare tactic to prevent me from thinking about boys and having sex). He never exposed their identities and only shared what he thought was important.

One story in particular stuck out the most—it was about a fifteen-year-old girl who was a prostitute. Her childhood started off in an abusive home and she found refuge on the streets of Las Vegas. She met a guy who she thought loved her but later learned that he was actually a pimp. Unfortunately, that relationship led her to prostitution at the age of twelve. By the age of thirteen, three diseases had consumed her: Chlamydia, syphilis, and herpes. She joined my father's program when she was fourteen and, once she did, her life started to turn for the better. She was placed in a loving foster home and started attending school again.

My dad's program saved that girl's life. This story taught me that not all "love" is good love. It also reminded me that our bodies are sacred and not meant to be shared with everyone. From that moment until now, I vowed to not engage in sex until I was married. Needless to say, sharing our purity with one another wasn't enough for my second crush and I to become boyfriend and girlfriend, so I was forced to move on.

During college, I met a Ghanaian-American man in my history class. He was very intelligent and funny. I stayed in the course for one week and later dropped the class but we were able to keep in touch on social media. Fast forward to the end of the semester, I moved back home to Las Vegas. When I moved, he shared with me he was interested in pursuing us further: He wanted me to be his girlfriend. Keep in mind, I informed him of my "status" and he told me that he accepted all of me. We dated long distance for one year and, during the second year, he decided he wanted to move to Vegas. He arrived in April 2012.

At first, I was nervous about being in the same city but, eventually, I enjoyed it. In May 2012, my father passed away. It was the worst timing for the relationship but my boyfriend was truly my best friend in that situation. He held me down like no other and, for that, I loved him. I was in love.

Shortly after in June 2012, his grandmother passed away and I made sure I was there for him. He was grieving so much that he became emotionally distraught and started crying. That night, he asked me to have sex with him. I thought about it and I honestly wanted to. I wanted to make him feel better than what he was feeling at that moment. I wanted to save him just like he saved me during my hard time. As I was fixing my mouth to answer him, the next phrase out of his mouth was "God will forgive you, please." At that moment, I realized I couldn't do it because it would've been for the wrong reason of pleasing the flesh. I also was uncertain if he really loved me or if it was just lust. I believed that there was a greater moment ordained for my husband and I to experience. So, my answer was no.

Months passed and the love of my life became cold and distant towards me. He was mean. He started taking drugs. One day, my womanly intuition said to call him, so I did. I called him and he answered, "Yeah." I asked him what was going on. He said, "I don't love you and I don't want you." I said "Okay. Why?" He gave me a stupid answer saying it was my mouth, implying that I always had an attitude. Honestly, my attitude was there, but he had told me he liked it! I then asked him, "Is it because of sex?" He was silent and didn't answer. Well, that was all the answer I needed.

I thought I was in love with that man and, if he just would've given me a little more time, it could've happened. Now began the cycle of defeat all over again. I was overwhelmed and I felt unworthy, lonely, ugly, and just not enough. That night, I was driving home and found myself so distraught that driving cautiously was impossible. Thankfully, I had enough strength to call my best friend. He calmed me down and, later that evening, met me at my house. He talked with me the entire evening and reminded me that I am loved, I am worthy, and I am enough.

How many friends can you call on that will show up and hold you accountable? How many of your friends can remind you that you are resilient and you will be restored in due time? Though it took a few years, I learned to forgive my ex-boyfriend and love him despite the situation. Regardless, that man was a good man, but he just wasn't the man for me. I learned to forgive myself for the self-sabotage and momentary failure to trust God in finding my lifetime partner.

Now in 2017, I am a better me because I practice self-love every day. I am constantly reminding myself of the principles that have helped me to SOAR and ROAR in life.

My SOARROARity™ Rules

Shine on in spite of your situation or circumstances.

Offer love as a solution for any situation.

Adversity is inevitable. Embrace it and know that you are a conqueror.

Rest. Don't be in such a hurry to go through life. Take moments to enjoy being among the living.

Reward yourself.

Ovation is on its way. Hustle hard and you will be rewarded.

Advocate for others as well as yourself. Support goes a long way and you never know when you may need it.

Royalty is a part of our foundation. We are queens and we deserve everything.

I discovered my own shine and inner beast, and I snatched my power back. The cycle was forever changed. I am wonderfully made and love-centered. I am Jocelyn "Love" Wallace.

SOAR~ROAR Reflection

1. In what ways have you been challenged to see yourself as loved?

2. What have you learned about love through your family dynamics?

3. Who in your family represents unconditional love and in what ways?

4. Can you think of a time when a pure love showed up for you just in the nick of time?

5. If you had only one person to depend on for a genuine love exchange, who would that be and why?

6. What's love got to do with your most pressing issues of life?

7. You are loved. In what ways do you feel loved by those who say they love you?

8. Call three people today and give them three reasons you will always love them unconditionally.

LASHONDA MOBLEY

YOU ARE DESTINY'S CHILD
Choosing to Triumph through the Trials

I was born in Oklahoma City, Oklahoma. Though I lived in a few other cities as a child, I primarily grew up in Oklahoma City. My father was in the military when I was younger so we moved out of state once or twice. My parents were pretty young when I was born, so things weren't always as structured as they would be in your typical family. But we made it through by the grace of God.

In this chapter, I'd like to share one incident in particular that influenced and impacted my life in a way that could have devastated me forever—*if* I had allowed it to. But that was not my destiny. Instead, I made a conscious effort to turn the page and live life on purpose.

When we are in the middle of chaos or a storm, it's easy for us to forget that we have a choice. We choose whether we fail or succeed, win or lose, triumph or travail. Ultimately, the choice, decision, and often the outcome are yours to decide. There are so many challenges we face as women, from being degraded and demeaned to overlooked and abused. We often lead various substantial roles in the lives of those around us. We are mothers, sisters, daughters, wives, entrepreneurs, business professionals, homemakers, worshippers, community leaders, teachers, and the list goes on and on.

But let's take a moment and reflect on the younger version of yourself.

Stop and envision her. What did she look like? How did she act? Who was she in comparison to who you are today? In what areas have you grown? What are some secret struggles she faced that beholds the very woman who so many know and love today? It's important for us to do these self-checks often to gauge the progress we've made, measure our success, track our triumphs, and know whether we've become all that we set out to be, especially during adversities and setbacks. If we don't remain mindful, we can find ourselves perpetually attempting to overcome life cycles that keep us bound and leave us feeling empty and desolate, repeating our pasts like a scratched CD that keeps skipping over and over again.

It is equally important to note that, when we are breaking cycles, progress and setbacks can go hand in hand, quite literally. We are constantly evolving, learning, and gleaning from one another and taking note of every lesson learned from our experiences. It would be nice to say we become master chefs after our first burnt meal, but that just isn't how it works. Each time we try to succeed, we get better and we eventually find our way out of the trials more refined and less likely to return to our desolate place.

Des·o·late (of a place): Deserted of people and in a state of bleak and dismal emptiness; feeling or showing misery, unhappiness, or loneliness.

I have lived in a desolate place several times. I was quite comfortable there. I had an impoverished mindset that continuously led to one poor decision after another and ended in shame. Like most people, I have said things like "I was dealt a bad hand" or "Why does this keep happening?" or the most notorious, "Why me?" There were times I wanted to quit because, for the life of me, I simply could not understand what on earth I was here for and what I was supposed to do with this life that seemed completely wrong from the very beginning.

There was a time when I was ashamed to say I was molested, cheated on, physically abused, stalked, divorced, a child of addicts, poor, grieved, motherless, and homeless. And right in the middle of these trials, it hit me like a ton of bricks: Suddenly, these challenges became laced with victory. My perception changed. I was no longer a victim of the situations that occurred in my life; in fact, most of them had very little to do with me at all. God allows us to endure such storms to encourage and inspire others to persevere in the face of controversy, to continue to live out our dreams regardless of what hand was dealt.

I chose to throw in the hand that was dealt to me and trade them for all new cards. My determination and drive to live the life that was intended for me would not allow me to simply quit. As children, we can't hand pick our lives. We don't get to choose our parents, siblings, nor some of the other things we encounter. But, as adults, we have opportunities to choose the lives we want. Again, that certainly is not to say that we'll always make the best or even remotely close to the right decisions. Lord knows I haven't. But today, I understand that many of the choices I made were direct effects of the trauma and chaos I was exposed to as a child.

As a young girl, I somehow developed a shy complex. I innately became suspicious of people and what they thought of me. I often felt odd or out of place. Growing older and facing different challenges in life, I became even more reserved. I had to be sure that everyone liked me, so I walked a fine line to ensure that people were pleased with me and who I was as a person. It was extremely important to me that I felt liked by almost everyone. In other words, I was a people pleaser, which made it easier for my perpetrator to select me.

Being molested at an early age impacted my worth in an unfathomable way. Sometimes, when it happened, it made me feel like I was a little princess. Afterwards, I felt nasty and undeserving of anything greater than what was offered. It was very confusing for a six-year-old girl. I remember getting certain privileges like being able to ride in the front seat while my other family members rode in the back, even though I was the youngest. I also got to choose if we were going for ice cream or candy. All the while, I was being groomed so that his hand could slip up my dress while I was in the front seat or so he could pick me up and get a quick feel while I chose which ice cream flavor I wanted.

He was a familiar family friend. No one suspected he'd do anything like this to me, but when I think back on it, he looked exactly like someone who would. He was obese and unkempt. He always had a different woman around, even though my dad and uncles seemed to have their significant others with them. When all the guys played dominoes, he never played with them, and he did not work out or play basketball like them either. I thought to myself, where does this guy fit in? Why is he always around? Oh yeah…he's the babysitter.

I remember being at his house, my family were in another room playing dominoes. I was in the kitchen alone with him. He had a cast on his leg at the time but somehow he managed to pick me up over the sink to show me the dogs in the backyard. The specific thing he wanted to show me was the dogs' penises, and then he, of course, showed me his. My mind doesn't allow me to remember any more specific details after that. One of the defense mechanisms I used as a young child was to block out some of the really hurtful parts. In my knowledge of trauma, people oftentimes will omit painful memories as a way to cope.

My perpetrator molested me for several years. As I got older, maybe nine or ten, I remember watching *The Oprah Winfrey Show* at my grandmother's house and feeling ashamed as Oprah and her guests began to expose their experiences with molestation. Wrong? What he was doing was *wrong*? No one ever told me that. I was told, of course, that it was *our* secret. But no one warned me that this wasn't *supposed* to be happening. Oprah and her guests were the first to ever tell me it was wrong.

I went into the linen closet in my grandmother's restroom, bawling and feeling desolate. When I came out, I finally got the courage to tell my mother what I had been dying to share with her: A family friend who everyone knew and trusted had been molesting me. She became furious as any caring mother would. She immediately contacted the family member who introduced us to my perpetrator. I felt so relieved to know that I would no longer have to see this disgusting man again and, more importantly, that he would no longer violate me and my body anymore.

But what I thought would lead to protection must have only served as a fair warning because he was still invited to be around my family, just not alone with *me* and he came around less frequently. I immediately thought, "Did I do something wrong?" I thought my job was to tell. Maybe I took too long to say something. Maybe I let him touch me for too many years.

The day was hot and sunny but quite gloomy as I saw his red truck pull up outdoors. I peeked out the window, but I stayed away because I did not want to see him. Just a few months after my conversation with my mother, another family member, who I loved dearly, told her mom that the same man started molesting her too! I was deeply saddened for her but was also outraged, because I told! I wanted to yell! I wanted to throw things! I wanted to fight! I told! I did what I was supposed to do! They listened, but the action was not severe enough to cause the sick man to stop. He was allowed to continue being around until he simply went to the next available little girl. It was only at that point our perpetrator was no longer welcome around the family in any manner.

This, as you can imagine, developed so many unanswered questions, insecurities, and justified comparisons in my immature mind. Why wasn't I important enough to make him go away when the abuse happened to me? Did they think the other girl was better than me? They must like or love her more. From there, the shyness further developed. I was firmly pushed away from people and felt I could not trust anyone. Furthermore, I wondered who I was as a person. I never really got the reassurance I needed from my parents to feel secure in who I was or learned what a real relationship should look and feel like. At that point, *his* touch, as wrong as it was, unfortunately became a premature encounter of what was supposed to be an experience shared with a person who truly loved me.

As a young adult, I had to unlearn what my perpetrator taught me about sexual encounters and relationships. I had to redefine how a man should be affectionate and intimate towards me. For a long time, I didn't like accepting things from men because I was groomed for so long that I felt like kindness meant I owed them something in exchange. I built up huge walls to protect myself. After every failed relationship, I would blame my perpetrator and my family because, if the abuse hadn't happened to me, I could have had a healthy relationship. I would remain single and abstain from sex for three years at a time when things didn't work out. It was during those times that I became extremely intolerable when someone did not meet my standards.

Later in life, I wanted answers as to how or why the abuse was allowed. I wanted to heal. I wanted to forgive everyone: Every adult who allowed the abuse and didn't protect me. I wanted to forgive my perpetrator. I earnestly believed they all wanted forgiveness and wanted me to heal too. So much so that they pronounced him dead.

He was dead? No! I wanted closure. I wanted to face him and let him know that I was no longer void of emotion in my relationships! The empty place he left in my heart was being filled with love that no man could ever misuse again. I wanted him to know that I now had a relationship with

Jesus Christ who is continuously healing me from my past wounds. Then, I wanted to ensure his salvation. That would have been the ultimate victory!

My family must've thought it would be easier for me to just move on with life if he was declared dead. Later, I found that he had a terminal illness and everyone *thought* he *would* die. I remember praying for him, asking God to restore his health so he would receive salvation. To my knowledge, he *is* still alive. I asked where he was so I could see and talk to him. But that information has yet to be revealed. Maybe one day soon, I will have the pleasure of facing him and telling him those three gentle words, "I forgive you."

Once I began to operate from a place of forgiveness instead of offense, healing really began to take place. Now, I can freely love a person regardless of the outcome. I choose to love wholeheartedly and without reservation. This is just one of the many obstacles I've made the conscious effort to overcome, to no longer be defeated, and to become the victor and not the victim through forgiveness and love. What the devil meant for evil, God turned around and made for my good: "And we know that all things work together for the good to them that love God and are called according to His purpose" (Romans 8:28).

Today, I have the awesome pleasure and privilege of empowering and encouraging others on a daily basis as a mental health therapist. While not everyone has dealt with sexual abuse before, I believe we all have situations in life that mold and shape us. Every struggle, feat, challenge, obstacle, triumph, and journey impacts us. Our environment makes up the very essence of who we are and what we stand for. It is the cause of why we believe what we believe and why we function the way we do.

As we evolve and shed our ugly but very necessary cocoons, we become the beautiful butterfly the world awaits. As the cocoon sheds, it doesn't fall off all at once, but bit by bit and piece by piece. We shed the layers of our yester-years as a little more light is allowed to come in. We must completely throw off all of the worn-out heaviness that we've been wearing so we can share our inner beauty with others who may be impacted by our transformation. We must tire of living in our cocoon. We can no longer get gratification out of being the victim. We can no longer be satisfied with accepting the hand that was dealt to us.

Maybe you were raped or molested. Maybe you are being abused or accused, or perhaps you are just on empty. You could be drained from giving so much of yourself that you have no time refuel, and you have become emotionally desolate. You are not alone. The very fact that you are reading this book and you are breathing indicates that there is life still within you and there are lives that you can impact. Your life can change. Decide today to live out loud! To no longer live in a shameful and empty place, and change your perception and your mindset. Say, "This didn't just happen *to* me. It happened *through* me." When we grasp this concept, we will have more control over our outcomes.

Say this with me out loud: I was destined to win! I will become all I desire to be! My past doesn't determine my future! I am loved! I am loveable! I embrace all of who I am! I am woman!

I A.M. W.O.M.A.N

Intensity: Live life intentionally and with intensity. What is your "it?" "It" is the thing that you cultivate and create to become someone who others in your life or circle can benefit from. For me, "it" was a life that was destined to fail according to society and its statistical findings. Those shortcomings, successes, and disappointments I now use to empower others. Show them that yes, God does bless mess!

Activate It: What are your dreams, goals, and gifts? Who do you aspire to become? Start developing the new and improved version of yourself by releasing your past and developing a blueprint for attaining those dreams, goals, and gifts.

Motivate It: Encourage yourself to actively pursue your dreams, goals, and aspirations by using positive affirmations daily. I call this "I am_____" statements: I am fearfully and wonderfully made in the image of God! I am a virtuous woman! I am strong and bold! I am relentless!

Withstand It: Trials and storms will come, so be prepared and be secure in the strength that lies within you.

Overcome It: Overcome the automatic negative thoughts that will come and try to tell you that you aren't worth it, you can't do it, or you don't deserve it. You are, you can, and you do!

Master It: Whatever your craft or trade, leave your mark. Become the best at what you do. Invest in yourself through time, attention, energy, and love for yourself!

Avoid It: Deliberately avoid the status quo, naysayers, and negativity. You can come up with the reasons, excuses, and all people in the world to blame for your lack of success, but don't waste any more time, space, or energy blaming others.

Nurture It: Just as a plant needs water, soil, and sun, so do your dreams, visions, and goals. Surround yourself with like-minded people who will help keep you focused and empowered.

As the butterfly bursts through the cocoon, it can take time for its wings to become fully developed. Once its wings are ready, the butterfly floats and soars through the air. Its mission is to feel the wind gliding against its wings, to be gently kissed by the sun, and to journey throughout life with purpose and fulfillment each day, while others marvel at how something that was once unpleasant is now strikingly breathtaking to gaze upon.

My SOARROARity™ Rules

Share your journey, trials, triumphs, successes, and failures. Someone needs to know that he or she isn't alone and your story could be the one to help change mindsets and lives. Your struggle wasn't just for you.

Operate in excellence. Whatever you do, do it with the spirit of excellence.

Accentuate your past. As bleak as some of it may be, find the golden moments and treasures that will remind you of the victory in your situation.

Reclaim who you are. You are not your past. You are just a byproduct of it.

Refine but never quit trying. Each time you try, you become better, greater, and more refined.

Optimize your time, space, and energy.

Aspire to be more than your past and greater than what people expect.

Be **R**elentless. Go after your dreams with everything you've got, regardless of what it looks or feels like.

SOAR~ROAR Reflection

1. When have you felt empty and void of emotion?

2. What caused you to dwell in a desolate place?

3. What are some of the hurtful areas of life you try to avoid dealing with in order to cope?

4. How do you cope with the difficulty of life reminding you of past hurts?

5. List some inventive ways for self-correcting in order to end cycles.

6. How can you begin living out loud starting today?

7. List some people who support you in positive change and spend more time with them.

8. If you feel you need professional help, make an appointment to see a professional as soon as possible.

TAMARA OMONDI

BLOOMING WHILE BARREN
Because We Were All Born to Birth

I had a pretty low-key life. I was born in the great state of Oklahoma, and grew up in the small town of El Reno. I spent all of my time with family, at church, or with one of the ladies from church when I wasn't in school. My parents provided a stable home, an incredible family bond, and a firm foundation in the Lord. Like most girls, I thought I would grow up, go to school, find a dapper dude who would sweep me off my feet, we'd marry, and we would choose when to expand our family.

Well most of my life happened that way, until it got to the part of beginning a family. After four years of marriage, being in my early twenties and having no natural success at getting pregnant, I realized something was off. Getting pregnant became an obsession. Now, I am forty years old and I still have never been pregnant; but, the journey I went on is so much deeper than simply being childless. Join me as I share how I've learned how to bloom through barrenness.

As a young girl and teen, I suffered attacks on my self-esteem. Most of it was done subtly and no real harm was meant by it, but it started a personal dialogue within me that was not positive. Being called "Miss Piggy" by family members and watching everyone nearly pass out from laughing is my first remembrance of feeling shame. Being too light skinned for some of my black friends, not living in the "Bottoms" (Northwest Community), and being the only black family who had a house built in a middle-class neighborhood were just some of the filters I began to see myself through. I always felt different, like I didn't belong. I never had many friends, I wasn't popular, and I certainly was not the teacher's pet. I was not first or last, but was simply average. I was a girl who felt invisible to the world. I had nothing special about me or awesome that I could offer of value. I battled with my weight and was "that weird girl" who always had to wear dresses. I was definitely the "peculiar" one who learned that being a background participant, not ruffling feathers and being obedient, would get me through life. No matter what I did or didn't do, I had one familiar feeling: Unworthiness.

I didn't realize this core issue until much later in life, but that single feeling of not being worthy created a cycle of unhealthy decisions, actions, and masks that I perfected to protect others from the truth that I felt crushed on the inside. At twenty-four years old, I was told that I was infertile and achieving pregnancy was pretty much impossible. That was the cherry on top of a lifelong battle of not being "good enough," not quite measuring up. I felt cheated. I felt that even God didn't find me valuable enough to allow me this desire to be a mother. He too wouldn't pick me and made my body flawed at the one thing it was designed to do: Produce.

I will never forget the day that my OB-GYN told me that she was referring me to an infertility specialist because everything she could do for me had been done and it had all failed. The specialist gave us our options of inter-uterine insemination (IUI) or in vitro fertilization (IVF), and told us that these options were not covered by insurance. I remember getting to the end of our very limited finances and having to ask my parents for help, then feeling like a failure after they gave up a few thousand dollars for procedures that ended up not being successful. That was the moment that everything inside of me shut down. I was a barren woman who was fat, broke, and unworthy. I absolutely wore the silent badge of shame and anger, even though I did what they told me to do. I lost weight, I took my temperature, I took the pills, I took injections in my belly, I spent my savings. I did things "right." I was educated. I was married. I had a three-bedroom home. I was ready, willing, and able to be the mother and nurturer I had been groomed to be since I was a child. I loved God and had worked in the Kingdom for years. But somehow, I still wasn't enough. And I took on that mentality—acceptance of my brokenness infiltrated my entire life in many other areas.

The definition of barren: Unproductive, infertile, unfruitful, sterile, bleak, lifeless, desert, pointless, futile, aimless, hollow, purposeless, unrewarding, useless. Showing no achievements. Empty of meaning or value.

Without realizing it, my entire life became barren. I lived my life with no real purpose except to just make it through the day. I was a nobody. Who'd notice or care anyway? But I also knew that nobody liked to be around a "Negative Nancy," so I learned to be fake in order to not make others shun me. I became a people-pleaser. To look at me, you wouldn't know a thing was wrong. I was great! I was positive! I laughed! I gave! I served! But, I ate to numb the pain of feeling like a failure. I stuffed myself to muffle the yearning in my womb.

Infertility is hard on relationships. You feel like you're a complete and utter disappointment to your spouse because you're unable to fulfill the things you talked about in those dating years. And he is not able to understand why you take the news of your friend's announcements of pregnancy so hard, or why it is especially difficult to attend, or better yet host a baby shower where the question on everyone's lips is "When are you going to have a baby?" If they only knew how that single question was like a meat cleaver to my already pummeled heart.

I found a way to balance the great happiness and joy I felt when my friends and family would announce another pregnancy with the disdain I felt when they would utter feelings of disappointment for getting pregnant "again." Pregnancy seemed *so* easy for everyone else, especially those who, in my opinion, didn't deserve it because they were not prepared or had conceived a child outside of ideal circumstances and were doing their best to hide it.

I stopped attending church. I stopped using my gift of song for Him because I knew that I was no longer in a space of true worship. I stopped opening my mail. I just stopped living to hide from the pain that was eating me up on the inside. I was in need of someone to see the real me. I needed someone to understand. I needed someone to relate. I needed someone to say, "I get it." I needed help but I didn't know how to ask for it, since I thought it would make me look weak. But most importantly, I couldn't take the rejection of someone not taking my feelings seriously or making me feel silly for feeling the way that I did.

Infertility for me was very much like experiencing an unexpected death. For as long as I could remember, I played a movie in my head of how my life would unfold. I had visions of my pregnant body, what it would be like to feel the baby move inside of me. I planned for my mother and me to go shopping and plan for the arrival of my little ones. I imagined and even made a spreadsheet of friends' and family's names, addresses, and phone numbers for hostesses to send out the cutest baby shower invites to. I had it all planned. I was ready. But what I was not prepared for was for *none* of that to happen. I didn't know how to maneuver my life with purpose because achieving motherhood was where I thought my worth resided.

Grief has five stages: denial, anger, bargaining, depression, and acceptance. Over the past nineteen years, I have gone through each of these stages to come to terms with ultimately accepting God's will for my life as it's unfolded thus far. Understanding why I was so down has helped me to work through my silent shame and start living the triumphant life that God always planned for me. But, I had to learn to get the focus off of me and onto Him.

Denial. In every desperate situation, there must be a certain hurting part of your brain that you shut off to keep hopefulness alive. I, to this day, am still hopeful that God will breathe on my body and allow me to experience the joys of creating and carrying a child. The difference is that I no longer let that one desire overwhelm my thoughts or define me as a woman.

Anger. I was sad, but my demeanor projected anger. I didn't know how to show the world my brokenness. I would verbally attack and hurt the people closest to me with my words. This pain was somehow their fault too. I was mad that they couldn't begin to understand how I felt and how their ignorance of it made me feel even more insignificant.

Bargaining. I would beg God for a child, saying, "God, if you just let me get pregnant, I will _____. If you allow me to have one child, I will _____. If you let me have a child I won't_____ anymore." I was trying to control God, just as I had tried to control this situation.

Depression. I couldn't show the world my pain, so I stuffed it with food. I would fill my mind with what I was going to eat next. I would literally eat lunch while thinking about dinner. I thought I was owed some sort of indulgence since "I did things right!" I went to work, went to school, paid the bills, helped out. I could do what I wanted to do during my down time. And eating and snacking wasn't hurting anyone, right? Nope! But it was killing me.

Acceptance. The cycle of silent self-destruction starts to get old. Stuffing yourself with things soon gets to a point where it's not enough. Food was no longer satisfying me. I had to find my hope. Restore my peace. Detach my self-worth from this single snap shot of my life and accept that I was disappointed that it didn't happen the way I had hoped, but my heart could be fulfilled and I could still become a mother to a child even if he or she was not from my womb.

For the first time in my entire life, I asked God to help me. I mean *really* help me. I couldn't fake it any longer. I couldn't keep putting the mask on. I could not answer the question *again* of "Why haven't you had a baby?" In those moments of deep sorrow and loneliness, God came and filled my womb with a desire to mother that was even greater. He told me to prepare even though I was broken, had no money, and my faith was nearly non-existent. I remember going to Babies R Us and seeing all of the pregnant mom's actively registering for their upcoming arrivals. So I did too. I received a Christmas bonus from my job in 2001 and I went and bought a floor model crib and changing table. I asked a friend to come over and help me put together this furniture. He agreed with a confused look on his face since there was no baby, no pregnancy, no nothing.

Over a five-month period, I purchased everything I needed. A car seat, package of newborn diapers, bottles, formula, swaddle blankets, bedding, and a week's worth of clothes (I thought fourteen outfits was enough for a newborn for a week—ha!). I stopped being pitiful and became powerful. My husband and I went to many adoption seminars and were turned down by many of them for different reasons, but mainly because of finances (or lack thereof). But my husband let me nest and didn't discourage me from preparing for this non-existent child. He let me just sit in that room and pretend. He probably thought I was losing my marbles, but I needed to do this because I was living in true expectation of a miracle. We had a home study completed and just waited.

Mother's Day weekend 2002, I invited my parents and my grandmother, Rosezelia Nelson, to my home for lunch and for her to see my new home. I hadn't told anyone about this nursery I had created. But my grandmother always told me to just believe for what I wanted. So, before they departed to head home, I had the courage to show them what I had been working on. Their reaction when I opened the door to that room was priceless. They all cried, including my daddy. Right then, it was as if they understood every sleepless night, every tear, every disappointment, every doughnut, every scar my body. But more importantly, they had the faith I didn't. In that room, they surrounded me and my grandmother put her hands on my tummy and said, "God, the work has been done. Now bring it to pass."

On August 4, 2002, at 10:04 a.m. (less than three months after that experience with my family in that room), my son came to us and was placed in my arms. Right then, I knew God loved me endlessly.

Now, you may be asking, what was the difference? Didn't you pray before? Didn't you believe before that God would help you get pregnant? Yes, I did. But the difference is that I had to stop telling God my dream and start living in His will. I started to soar in the fullness of God when I stopped trying to direct God and started trusting Him. I started to roar when I accepted that there was more than one way to produce. I was fertile and was designed to blossom.

My SOARROARity™ Rules

Surrender: To His will. To His way. To His Timing. To His Options.

Obey: I had to stop begging and start being obedient.

Action: I had many, many plans, but I never took a step of faith and lived in expectation of the promise. I kept telling God what I wanted, but it was when I started journaling and presenting my plans and heart's desires to God, that those thoughts became prayers, which ultimately became my petition to Him.

Repent: I had to ask God to forgive me for all of the hurt I created, all of the unnecessary grief I caused myself and all of the people around me. I had to forgive myself.

Radical: I had to be radical in my thinking and my boldness. I couldn't live in a daydream. I had to actively stay aware of every thought, action, and deed.

Overcome: It was necessary to overcome the thoughts and feelings of shame and worthlessness.

Atmosphere: I learned that I was responsible for the atmosphere I allowed my spirit to reside in. If I had a negative thought, I had to swiftly recognize it and change my atmosphere to keep my mind in the place of worship and expectancy. That automatically brought about peace and hope, and gave me that unspeakable joy that I always heard of but truly never experienced.

Relationships: I had to find my refuge in Jesus. Not my husband. Not doctors. Not friends. I had to learn who my source was and develop a true relationship with Him. I had to be in communion with Him at all times because it is easy for your faith to waiver during the adoption process. Without this component, none of the other things would matter. I had to submit, surrender, and surround myself with Him and trust His leading and guiding, especially when I was scared.

During my journey of infertility, I found that I was able to bloom while barren when I just let go of me and held onto Him. Over the years, I have learned that I am not barren. I am actually incredibly fertile. God needed me to endure this pain to really get to a place of submission so that I would not be easily broken when faced with difficult battles in the future, ranging from divorce and illness to becoming a single mother.

God wanted me to see that there are many ways to give birth. I birthed my son, not from my womb, but from every inch of my heart. I have birthed multiple businesses and a non-profit organization whose ripple effects are felt across the country with a vision to touch hurting people. I am able to bloom right where I'm planted, because God is my Creator, my Source, and my Truth. He handcrafted me and gave me limitless fertile ground to plant seeds of hope, opportunity, and unfailing love. I was put on this earth to help be a mid-wife to other people's dreams and desires, and to be an example that God wastes no experience, no hurt, no disappointment, and no person. There is purpose even in pain, if we just learn to lean into Him and trust that He will bring us through all seasons of our lives better, stronger, and wiser.

The Shift from Barren to Blossom

So how does one blossom while in a broken, shameful, and shattered place?

Build a tribe of people who believe in you, support you, and will be there for you when you're in a slump. This tribe will remind you of your why and encourage you to get up and continue on.

Love until others ask you why. Love when it's hard. Love when you don't understand. Love without conditions. Give the love that you didn't deserve when you were in your lowest places.

> [17] that Christ may dwell in your hearts through faith; that you, being rooted and grounded in love, [18] may be able to comprehend with all the saints what is the width and length and depth and height— [19] to know the love of Christ which passes knowledge; that you may be filled with all the fullness of God.
>
> *— Ephesians 3:17-19 (NKJV)*

Operate in the gifts that God has given you.

> [4] For as we have many members in one body, but all the members do not have the same function, [5] so we, being many, are one body in Christ, and individually members of one another. [6] Having then gifts differing according to the grace that is given to us, let us use them: if prophecy,

let us prophesy in proportion to our faith; ⁷ or ministry, let us use it in our ministering; he who teaches, in teaching; ⁸ he who exhorts, in exhortation; he who gives, with liberality; he who leads, with diligence; he who shows mercy, with cheerfulness.

— Romans 12:4-8 (NKJV)

Serve God by working in His Kingdom, serving others, and serving in the community.

Stand in expectancy that God can and will use you and your abilities for His glory. Stand in the gap for others who are also in pain. Stand in the truth that you are a victor and not a victim.

Be **O**riginal. Many may be doing similar things that you're putting your hands to, but there is only one you. Be authentic and faithful to the call and trust the process that God has called you to. But once you put your hand to it, don't look back (Luke 9:62). Do not start comparing your call, vision, and results to those of others. Many are called and few are chosen, but many choose not to take their rightful place, show up, and be accounted for.

⁶² But Jesus said to him, "No one, having put his hand to the plow, and looking back, is fit for the kingdom of God."

— Luke 9:62 (NKJV)

Multiply your reach by leveraging your gifts and talents so that the overflow of your offerings is limitless. You can only do this by keeping your relationship with God intact and preserving Him as the main priority of your being.

> "⁸ But other seed fell on good ground and yielded a crop that sprang up, increased and produced: some thirtyfold, some sixty, and some a hundred."
>
> — *Mark 4:8 (NKJV)*

SOAR~ROAR Reflection

1. Where are you barren in your life?
2. Are you suffering silently?
3. What is the root cause of your pain?
4. Are you self-medicating? If so, how?
5. What are your action steps to gain clarity?
6. What are your gifts and talents?
7. Have you talked to God to see how you can use your gifts and talents to serve Him and others?
8. What detailed plan have you written down and submitted to God to begin the budding process of your blossom?

KINDRA LOWERY

THE INCARCERATION OF INVISIBILITY
Bringing Light to Shadows

The incarceration of invisibility has two sides. On one hand, you have the shackles of being held bondage by your invisibility and the issues and negativity that ensue as a result. On the other hand, you have the posture of victory that is assumed because you now hold captive the things that once had you bound. From *captive* to *captain*!

Grab a hot cup of tea and your favorite blanket and experience my journey as I go from captive to captain, bringing light to shadows.

I've been called by many names over the years: Wife, mother, homemaker, and children's ministry teacher. My children in summer camp called me "Mrs. K," and for some of them, I was a counselor and mentor. I homeschooled my children, so I was their teacher. I've had people tell me that I was an Evangelist. I would look at them and smile, but think to myself "Yeah right, you missed it. God is talking about somebody else."

For a season, I was completely content with being the best wife and mother that I knew how to be. After five years or so, I began to feel incomplete, like there was something else I was supposed to be doing. Don't get me wrong—being a wife, mother, and homemaker were some of my greatest accomplishments! If I had it to do all over again, the only thing I would change is the fact that I lost myself. My home was in order. I was able to prepare home-cooked meals at least five days a week for my family. I could pray, praise, and worship God without distractions. I'd also set the atmosphere before my husband and children came home.

My pastor would preach messages about the importance of knowing one's purpose. There is a peace and confidence that comes with knowing and walking in your purpose. I would weep. I didn't have a clue about my identity, let alone God's purpose for my life. I volunteered for several different ministries, hoping that this would help me discover my purpose or true place in ministry. I didn't grow up in church like my husband's family or most of the people I served alongside had. However, I made myself available for boundless service to the Lord.

During my diligent service, I served in the following areas of ministry: Evangelism, intercessory team, children's ministry teacher, hospitality, and the praise and worship department. I also volunteered in our ministry's corporate office, serving my pastor and first lady weekly in whatever capacity they needed.

Still, after years of service, I didn't know my purpose. And, although being active in ministry forced me out front, I often felt invisible. How is it that you can be openly exhorting God's people and still feel invisible and inadequate? Until recently, I didn't know why. The Bible says in John 10:10, "The thief cometh not, but to steal…" The enemy meant to steal my innocence, my peace, my confidence, and my self-worth.

He wanted me to remain hidden with scales over my eyes as if I had scotoma (blindness or blocking out of reality). Then, I wouldn't be able to see myself, or the truth regarding who I am. More importantly, I would not see who my Father is. But the devil is and has always been a liar and a father himself of lies. But God has removed the scales from my eyes. God revealed to me the thing that has had me incarcerated for so many years. God exposes the things in us that prevent us from moving forward so that we ourselves can get rid of them. Once we can clearly see, we can then course correct and release what's holding us captive.

I tell my children all the time to pray for anyone who is unfriendly to or around them, because there is a root to every behavior. God recently revealed the root to every unfruitful thought or feeling I've ever had. When I was six years old, I was first fondled and then raped by my nineteen-year-old cousin. Some of what he did was in my parents' own home. He would act as if he wanted to tuck us all in and say goodnight, and then stick his fingers in me underneath the covers while my baby sister laid next to me. Because he told me that I was the one who did something wrong and would get in trouble, I was too scared to say anything to my parents. It was my three-year-old brother who eventually told my mom.

It's been thirty-six years. Why was I fearful, paralyzed, and struggling with the idea of attending another cousin's funeral? I knew it was the ceremony for *his* sister, whom I loved dearly. But I didn't want to see *him*. I kept asking myself, "Why are all these images replaying in my mind now?" I can still see the red and blue lights that he turned on, as if he were setting some type of mood with a six-year-old baby. Yes, you read it right: This nineteen-year-old man took a six-year-old into his room, laid her down on his bed, and turned on soft lights.

So many times, I've questioned why this happened to me. Why didn't I scream or feel anything emotionally while it was happening? Why did I just lay there, while he made my five-year-old sister stand at the door and watch? My parents were right down the hall. Many family members knew what he had done. Why did they act as if nothing happened? Couldn't they see that I was acting out? We are all quick to highlight the unwanted behavior of little girls: Calling them "fast" or saying they will soon end up pregnant. No one addresses the root cause.

It wasn't until I had to face my offender at my cousin's funeral that I realized what he had done to me still had some type of effect on me. When I began writing my story and doing research on children who had been sexually abused, I realized that I too suffered the same long-term effects of what had happened to me. I didn't know how to externalize the abuse. What my cousin did made me feel worthless, damaged, defective, unqualified, inadequate, and invisible.

I struggle with trust and, at times, my emotions are all over the place. I had, and on occasion, *still* have horrible stomach pains. These symptoms are said to be long-term effects of the trauma. Lack of forgiveness not only holds you in bondage, but it can manifest itself in the physical. The stress from it can ultimately kill you! Has there ever been a time when there was something or someone you had a hard time forgiving? When I'm holding on to bitterness or anger, I feel it most in my neck, shoulders, and back. At times, I can't move the top half of my body at all. When it gets to that point, I pray and ask God to show me who I need to forgive.

I am reminded of the story of Tamar in 2 Samuel 13. Tamar was King David's daughter. She was not only beautiful herself, but was always arrayed in beautiful garments. Her garments of diverse colors represented her being the King's daughter and her being a virgin. Long story short, after being raped by her brother Amnon (David's firstborn son), Tamar put ashes on her head, rent her clothes, and remained desolate (barren, laid waste, or not producing) in her other brother Absalom's house.

Neither David nor Absalom said anything good or bad to Amnon about what he'd done to his sister. In fact, after Tamar had been raped, Absalom saw his sister, crying, clothes rent, and first asked her if her brother Amnon had been with her. How did he know? The Bible doesn't say that God revealed to Absalom what happened to his sister. Was there a pattern? Signs or behaviors that Absalom had seen but never mentioned? Can you believe he had the nerve to tell Tamar to hold her peace and to remind her that Amnon was her brother?

Even today, why is it that so many families don't talk about these types of offenses? Don't they know that, without help, these babies, girls or boys, are left to try and sort out sexual, emotional, and physical pains all by themselves? Feelings that they don't understand.

It wasn't until I began to do the research for my contribution to this book, that I realized that I was Tamar. I held myself captive for thirty-six years and was totally unaware of it. I even wanted to abort my assignment to complete this contribution. The enemy truly comes to destroy. Isn't it awesome how God always sends the perfect word for us right when we need it?

My pastor said that some of the most successful people in the world were once the biggest quitters. They had to quit bad habits and stinking thinking, which we normally verbalize. I realized that my thoughts spoken would become my reality, for as a woman thinks in her heart, so is she. I chose to change my words to reflect the truth of who God says I am. Years ago, another pastor of mine taught this awesome series for our women's Bible Study. He talked of the importance of *knowing* our value: Knowing that we *are* valued and *valuing* what we know. Our identity is found only in God. The closer we get to Him and the more we get to know about Him, the more we find out about ourselves.

Isaiah 52:1, 2, 7, 9, & 11 says:

1. "AWAKE, AWAKE; put on thy strength, O Zion; put on thy beautiful garments, O Jerusalem, the holy city; for henceforth there shall no more come into thee the uncircumcised and the unclean."

    - We must wake up and put on our strength, "the whole armor of God" (Ephesians 6:10-18). If we measured our destiny with the offense (whatever has happened to us), they could never compare! Our destiny and purpose are too important. If we don't let go, forgive, and move on, we'll delay our own destiny.

2. "Shake thyself from the dust; arise, and sit down, O Jerusalem; loose thyself from the bands of thy neck, O captive daughter of Zion."

    - We have the authority and power to loose ourselves.

7. "How beautiful upon the mountains are the feet of him that bringeth good tidings, that publisheth peace; that bringeth good tiding of good, that publisheth salvation; that saith unto Zion, Thy God reigneth!"

    ▸ This is what this book is all about! When we share God's word, love, and sacrifice, we're no longer silenced. We use our stories, experiences, and failures (which ultimately ended up being our victories in Christ) to encourage and uplift others. We're bringing tidings of good! We are publishing salvation and basically saying to our communities and to the world, "Our God Reigneth"!

9. "Break forth (out into the open) into joy, sing together, ye waste places of Jerusalem: for the Lord hath comforted his people, he hath redeemed Jerusalem."

    ▸ Break (annul or separate) ourselves from anything that keeps us from moving forward. Breaking away from anything is a violent process, but it's necessary.

    ▸ Identify what our waste places are: Bitterness, negative thinking, fear, doubt, poor self-image, anger, jealousy, etc.

    ▸ We have the ability to SOAR, but those waste places clip our wings.

11. "Depart (leave) ye, depart ye, go ye out from thence, touch no unclean thing; to ye out of the midst of her; be ye clean, that bear the vessels of the Lord."

- Get out of the midst of every negative person, thought, or situation.

- Repent and be ye clean. 1 John 1:9 says, "If we confess our sins, he is faithful and just to forgive us our sins, and to cleanse us from all unrighteousness." We cannot go to God any kind of way—we must be clean!

- Know that you are a chosen vessel of the Lord.

God placed me in a family full of so many awesome gifts and abilities, all of which are out front. Some are pastors, evangelists, strong vocalists, awesome songwriters, and authors. One day, out of nowhere, I thought to myself, "I have become all of those things!" Most people know that I would rather be behind the scenes, but I now see that God never meant for me to stay behind the scenes.

Out of all of my siblings, I'm the firstborn. I was born to be a leader. But because of the poor perception I had of myself, I was unable to recognize that part of my destiny. I learned that our leadership is, indeed, in service. My brother-in-love put it more simply, "A leader is just a servant that is out front." Just the other day, I was thinking that on every job I've ever held, I started out as an assistant. Over time and without promotion, I wound up (by default) taking on managerial responsibilities. Its' amazing how you can exhibit leadership qualities and responsibilities without the title. We were all born to lead in some way. We were chosen by God, fearfully and wonderfully made, and complete *in* Him. "For *freedom*, Christ has set us free; we can stand firm, and not be subject again to the yoke of slavery" (Galatians 5:1).

It's imperative that we see ourselves for the individuals God has purposed us to be—beloved and complete (lacking nothing)—, and seek God for His plan for our lives. It is essential that we spend time getting to know God, which is the only way we'll really ever know our worth! We must also learn how to let go, because our destiny is far more important than any offense, and know without question that nothing can happen to us unless God allows it.

Wake up and put on your strength daily, whether in worship, time spent reading or listening to His word, or through conversing with positive people who want God's best for your life. This is how I reload myself and replace my negative thinking. In everything, we must remain thankful and optimistic. Why? First, because He says so: "In everything we are to give thanks." This changes your perception of what it is you go through. His joy is our strength and His strength is made perfect in our weakness. His Word not only brings us peace, but also lights our path! We are not alone and God is still masterfully crafting us.

Let patience have her perfect work, because then and only then will we be perfect and entire, wanting nothing. We are not just works in progress, but completed works in further progress, confident that He who has begun His good work in us will complete it until the day of Jesus Christ. When God gives me something to do, I will move with alacrity, confidence, and no fear, knowing that my steps are ordered by Him. I won't be silent, but I will be a voice for the voiceless. I will be their trumpet! I will trumpet that our latter is all that matters.

My SOARROARity™ Rules

See yourself as the woman or man God has purposed and created you to be: Take your focus off everyone else.

Order: Defined as a "state of peace, a definite plan," or God's plan for your life. God promised to keep him in perfect peace whose mind stays on Him, His word, and His promises.

Appraise: To estimate, determine, know the worth of. It is vital that we get to know who He is, how important He is (it's in Him that we live, move, and have our being), and know our worth!

Release: To free from confinement, bondage, obligation, pain, or anything that restrains. Like the leaves on a tree that must be shed every fall, we must release anything that prevents us from growing or moving forward, so that we may bear new life.

Reload: Something that was once full must be emptied and filled up again. We must come before Him empty, because something full can never be filled.

Optimism: We must have the expectation, trust, assurance, hope, confidence, and certainty (faith) that, with God, all things are possible.

Alacrity: Defined as "an eager willingness, often with quick, lively action." We either allow fear to keep us from walking into the things God has given us to do, or we don't have any stick-to-it-ness. We quit before God has a chance to manifest His promises. When God gives you something to do, get after it quickly, with confidence!

Radiate: To send out rays of heat or light, to spread happiness and love, to send forth from a center (God being our center), to shed or to blaze. Our road should be heard beyond the four walls of what we call the church, never constrained by religious rigidity, but beaming with the freedom that comes with walking in God's purposeful plan and will for our lives. Light shines brightest in darkness. If all we're doing is preaching to each other, then all we are is a bunch of high beams in an already well-lit room!

I am no longer a prisoner of the fear that once gripped me. Praise be to God! He ended it quickly. Why? My mind was and is stayed on Him. I am on my face before Him and pray to embrace any day. I am amazed by the way that He slew anything that could potentially cause a delay in the plans He made. I now see everything He allowed me to overcome as a victory. The blessed in me brings out the best in me. I'm forever grateful He tested me and arrested me in the blessed essence of His presence. Yes, victory *is* my destiny!

SOAR~ROAR Reflection

1. Who are you? Do you know God's plan for your life?

2. Do you know how valuable you are to God? Describe your value to Him.

3. Who is God to you?

4. Have you taken the time to appraise God's importance in your life? If not, do so now.

5. What things (waste places) do you need to release or shed?

6. Do you empty yourself daily? How?

7. When God gives you a directive, do you move quickly? Give examples.

8. Are you a beaming light, effecting change in your sphere of influence? Or are you a dim and flickering light whose brightness has been hidden beneath years of inclement weather and storms (fear, bitterness, doubt, feelings of inadequacy, etc.)? Explain.

ASHLEY Q. TILLMAN

DETERMINED DESPITE DOUBT
Failure Is Not Final…

I was born and raised in Las Vegas. I had a pretty good childhood as the only girl of four children (I have two older brothers and one younger brother). Though both my parents worked, my father was the primary provider and my mother's responsibility was to take care of the family. My mother raised me to be *perfect*. I came up in the "children are to be seen and not heard" era. I was expected to speak well, dress well, and be a solid representation of a poised young lady. The weight of what my mother thought my life should look like was placed on my shoulders at a very early age. It bore nothing I really wanted for myself but everything she thought I needed.

Soon enough, I would come to realize that carrying the weight of what others want for me would become the theme of my life, and the fear of letting others down would become commonplace as well. Eventually, I came into my own truth and I found the will and determination to live my best life. Let me share with you how that came to be.

Like most young girls, I was raised to be a lady. My mother and grandmother saw to it that I was given grave instructions on how to carry myself. Both were prideful women and took perception very seriously, so I had no choice but to do the same. Throughout my formative years, I grew to lean on what my mother thought was best for me, rather than what I thought for myself. She was always right there to tell me what was right, fight my battles, and be my voice, even when her voice did not align with mine. What I thought and felt were never important because she already had it all figured out. It never occurred to me that I was never given the chance to form my own identity or use my voice, to discover who I was or what I liked.

At the same time, my mother expected me to have it all together because she had provided me with all the tools. So, I got comfortable with going with the flow and living life the way others thought I should. I began to suppress my true feelings and hide my emotions. No matter how I felt, I would suck it up and press on. I had to be okay. I could not fail. Period.

So, if you would have asked me ten years ago where I would be as a thirty-year-old woman, I would have sounded off with an answer that embodied success and nothing less. I envisioned having an accounting career, owning a beautiful home, being married to an amazing man, and having a child or two. This is what my success looked like for me through the eyes of others. I just knew my life would be well put together. And honestly, it was obtainable; all I had to do was listen to all the great advice that was thrown my way: Stay on track. Stay motived. Live above the negative influence. Surround yourself with the right people. I can hear my mother's words so clearly.

But I quickly realized that none of those things would be easy. There were two things that were never made clear to me when I began to plan my life as an adult woman. I think these pieces of very valuable advice would have helped me so much. I'm sure they would have kept me going. And those are: It's okay to fail sometimes and it's okay to not be okay.

I know you're probably thinking that this should have been a no-brainer. But when you're trying to live on the right path, attempting to make everyone proud (including yourself), the mere thought of failure can be frightening. I mean deathly frightening. My breakdown finally came when I was in my sophomore year of college whilst working full time. I was in a long-term relationship with my high school sweetheart and providing for myself, the way everyone thought I should. I was on the right track and, from the outside looking in, I had it all together.

There was just one problem: Underneath it all, I was miserable. It was all too much and I didn't know how to admit that without sounding like a failure. I couldn't ask for help because that would mean I didn't have it figured out like everyone thought I did. It didn't matter that my relationship was riddled with disrespect and infidelity—at least I had one. It didn't matter that my grades in school weren't the best—C's get degrees. It didn't matter that I hated my job—at least I was working toward a career and making more money than most people my age. I hated my life and, at that point, most of the people in it. And it all began to show.

I didn't graduate college on time, which was a dead giveaway that I was not on track in school. I was on the brink of being fired from my job, which was a dead giveaway that I was not performing at work. My relationship abruptly ended, which was a dead giveaway that my partner and I were not happy. I would give people an attitude out of this world and look a hot mess, which were dead giveaways that I did not have it all together. And when everyone began to realize what I had known all along—that my life was falling apart around me—I reacted like any person in denial would: I got mad. Mad at myself for living a lie. Mad at my mother who judged me way too much and always had something to say about the way I lived my life. Mad at my ex-boyfriend for being disrespectful and unfaithful. Mad at my friends for not helping me (even though I always told them that I was okay). I was just mad.

But once my cover was blown, I no longer had to live the "lie" of perfection. I will admit, that was the most freeing moment of my life. And in that moment, I realized the only person that I could be mad at was *me*.

I took a sabbatical from school. I was barely doing enough to remain employed at work and was just getting by. I was blessed enough to have a co-worker at the time who saw what I was going through. She got real with me about what needed to happen next and held me accountable. She suggested I talk to someone—a very professional someone. A therapist. At first, I was offended. I was going through something but I didn't need "that kind of help." Here I was (again), not wanting to admit I was not okay and insisting that things weren't as bad as they seemed. But this good friend of mine did not let me off the hook. She knew me better than I knew myself at the time and how stubborn I could be. She reminded me that everything happens for a reason and that going to counseling didn't mean that I was crazy; it meant that I wanted to get my life back on track.

So, I went. I made the decision to stop caring so much about what others thought and to start caring more about what I thought and wanted for myself. Getting an objective point of view from someone I could be open and honest with, for the first time in my life, was the best thing I could have done. Through the job I hated (go figure), I was able to secure four sessions with my therapist. Four sessions that opened me up to the notion that failure is a very real part of life and success. I quickly learned that what I was going through was not meant to break me; it was meant to grow, shape, and prepare me for the life I wanted. I saw that, not only was I in denial, I was also battling self-esteem issues, family issues, and a host of other issues I had suppressed and decided I didn't have to deal with while attempting to live a perfect life.

My therapist was so real. She did not hold back. She told me everything I needed to hear, everything I did not want to hear, and some things I had heard before. Sometimes, you don't listen because the information may be coming from people that you no longer trust, so even good advice can fall on deaf ears. I discovered that everything I had been through was all necessary to get me to the point of realizing that all I wanted, needed, and desired was within reach and it was up to me to obtain them. As I worked through the hard stuff with my therapist, I also began to discover that, eventually, I would have to take back control of my life and start making my own decisions. Decisions independent of what my parents thought, my friends thought, and anyone else that did not have to live my life thought. I gradually got back on track and began to see that life was all about making the most of the now while working towards the future. My goal was to remain determined no matter what. This occurred in steps.

1) Face the truth

My first step was facing the truth about *me* and what that meant for myself. I discovered that each person's truth is his or her own. What I believe, what I want, what I desire, and what I feel is my choice—they have nothing to do with any other person. No one is responsible for my happiness or my truth but myself. For example, my mother would always tell me what it took to be successful and even what success looked like and, for a long time, I believed what she said. I believed I had to talk a certain way, dress a certain way, and even entertain certain relationships that made me uncomfortable. But her truth about life and success were not mine. While I do hold on to some of the valuable things that I've been taught throughout my life, I now know that I don't have to accept everything that has been shared with me as law over my life.

Just because someone offers you advice doesn't mean you must take it. You don't have to accept anything anyone says as fact if you don't want to. Your truth and the truth of others may be very different, and that is okay.

2) Find you and accept her

Next, I had to find out who I was and accept *her*. I think this was the toughest aspect for me to conquer because I was the person who took what everyone thought of me, good or bad, and made it the gospel of my life. I was the woman who thought I was beautiful because others said I was beautiful. I thought I was intelligent because I exemplified all the things that people thought an intelligent woman did. I thought I was selfish because I didn't do everything that people asked of me and that's what they would label me.

Through one of my sessions with my therapist I quickly learned that these were the signs and symptoms of an insecure person. I was insecure and I didn't even realize it. I relied on the compliments of others to determine how I felt about myself. I let others mold me into what I was incapable of molding myself into and I let how others perceived me become the labels I would eventually use to describe myself. I thought I was a host of things but I never took the time to sit down and ask myself, "Who are you, really?"

When you neglect to determine who you are, what you are, and what that means to you, you leave yourself open for others to determine those things for you. Get honest with yourself. Ask the tough questions about what makes you happy and what doesn't. You must decide what you will accept and what you won't. You must determine what your values are, what you feel is right, and what you perceive as wrong. And the most important piece to all of this is that you must believe yourself regardless of what anyone else may think of you. It was tough, and I still struggle with this today, but I will no longer be defined by how others see me.

3) Failure is okay

I had to face the truth about failure. The act of failing has such a negative stigma tied to it that no one thinks of it in a positive manner. I had to unlearn everything about failure to understand that the failing does not mean you are a *failure*—the actions that follow failing is what determines if you have failed. On the road to success, you will fail many times but you must learn to start seeing each time as a blessing or a lesson. You must remain optimistic about failure. That is the only way to not let it get to your heart or your head. I believe that, sometimes, God allows us to fail at things to show us that what we are attempting to succeed at isn't right for us. Or maybe we are going about it the wrong way and we need to try it differently. In either instance, we immediately learn that what we are attempting to do is not fruitful or healthy for us.

Failure also tends to build you up mentally and assist in your growth. I learned that, if everything goes as you plan it, then you never get the chance to build your perseverance muscle. This very important muscle allows you to keep going despite unfortunate circumstances and is strong enough to push you through defeat. This muscle is also necessary to carry the weight of life when failure knocks you down momentarily. I got really good at using my perseverance muscle and it continues to help me accept who I am.

4) Learn to let go

Once I accepted my truth and who I was, I knew it was time to let go of all things and people who I decided were toxic to my life. And I mean everything and everyone. I was determined to live a more positive life so that meant things had to change and anything that did not align with my new way of thinking had to go. Whenever you get to the point where you discover that something or someone no longer serves you in a positive manner, it is okay to detach. This doesn't mean you don't love the person or that you don't care about a certain thing; it just means that your time with that person or thing has expired.

Remember, every time you say "yes" to someone else's happiness over your own, you give that person power over your life. I was done giving my power to others. I let go of a few close friends and a job that allowed me to make a comfortable living. I let them go because, not only did they stress me tremendously, but the way I was being treated did not align with the new standard I set for myself. To get to my "yes" and what a happy and fulfilling life looked like to me, I had to say "no" to certain things and make sacrifices. I was done being everything to everyone else. Sometimes, I feel that women get so wrapped up in attempting to be all the things that others want us to be that we forget to just be ourselves. Once I let go of all the people and things that I was allowing to hold me down, I began to truly soar in my purpose.

Getting to this point was no easy task, but once I accepted my truth, discovered who I am and what I desire, and finally learned that it is okay to fail, it became so much easier to soar with assurance. What success looks like to you will change over time as you change, but your will to succeed and be the best must remain constant. Despite the doubts of others, I now roar with greatness because I know that failure is not final for me.

My SOARROARity™ Rules

Sound off: I let my voice be heard.

Own the truth: My truth is mine. I own it and stand proud in it, no matter what.

Acceptance: I accept who I am, just as I am.

Redeem Strength: I redeemed the strength necessary to make my own decisions about my life.

Remain Resilient: No matter how tough life gets, I remind myself that I am just as tough and I keep going.

Optimism: What you think, you become. I overcame the negative thoughts I had about myself to shine light on the positives. I am determined to remain optimistic despite circumstances.

Attitude: I realized that my attitude was going to determine my altitude so I had to check myself. I began to approach life with an attitude of gratitude.

Rest in certainty: All things will work out the way God intends them to. My faith allows me to rest easy knowing that this truth is certain. God makes no mistakes.

What I thought success would look like in my sophomore year of college versus what I think it is now is so different. I didn't even know who I really was then so it was impossible to determine what I wanted. I look back on the things I went through and what it took to get me past my trials, and I am confident in knowing that I have what it takes to be great. This doesn't mean I won't get derailed at times; but it does mean that I will remain steadfast in the faith I have in God and in myself. If you stay committed to who you are and what you want, no one can stop you. Remain determined without a doubt because failure is not final unless you say so.

SOAR~ROAR Reflection

1. Do you have a confident sense of self?

2. Do you struggle with expressing your true thoughts?

3. Can you effectively deal with your emotions? If not, why?

4. Are you able to make conscious decisions without the opinions of others?

5. What do you do to remain focused despite the doubts you may have about your abilities?

6. Do you have a healthy support system?

7. Have you taken a realistic inventory of your inner circle to determine who belongs in your life and who does not?

8. What are some of the positive approaches you use to block out negative self-talk and remain determined to soar?

TIANNA R. LEWIS

BEING IS BELIEVING
How to Conquer Fear and Bring Your Dreams to Fruition

If you are reading this, please excuse me. I prefer to skip over the pleasantries for now, since being as least transparent as possible is just *easier*. Trust me, I am fully aware of the consequences of such cold behavior. I am no stranger to loss as a result of my being a closed book rather than an open novel. But let me assure you: I have had plenty of practice guarding my heart at the expense of others.

I often ask myself, "When did I first learn to fear?" Was it when I suffered a concussion at the hands of men in uniform, resulting in my toothless smile? Was it when my virginity was stolen from me by a group of young men (who I pray today don't have daughters of their own)? Perhaps it was much earlier than that, when my parents divorced and changed the perception of my world forever.

The truth is, I have been wrong on so many levels about where my longtime fear of living freely and confidently has stemmed from. If you consider yourself to be a fearless superior being, then I suggest that you do not waste your time and skip this chapter altogether. To those of you struggling with fear and doubt in various areas of your life, I encourage you to find refuge in my story. Listen to my message: Perfection is a myth and the only true path to any semblance of perfection in this life is to find, keep, and spread your peace.

I learned how to engage in fear the same way that all of us do: With the planting of a seed. At age five, I lived in Bakersfield, California, with my (at the time) happily married mother and father. I was in a fairly small first-grade class, and absolutely adored my teacher. Although her name has left my memory, her Stepford wife appearance is forever embedded in my mind. After all, I have her to thank for the many years I wasted, walking in fear.

"Don't touch me," I said to the immature young boy who sat behind me and annoyingly poked at my back for his own selfish amusement. Reading time was normally exciting and thrilling for me, especially since my mother read to me every night before bed. However, on this particular day, my moment of imagination and adventure was threatened and my patience tested.

"I said, *stop* touching me!" My patience had come to a halt. Apparently, so did my teacher's who had not properly assessed the situation. When I raised my hand to seek her assistance, she asked, "What's wrong with you?" Unaware of her condescending tone, I told her that the young man would not stop touching me. Of course, he denied it, leading my teacher to respond to me by saying, "Something is wrong with you." Her voice echoed. Her lie echoed. My young ears served as the mountaintop upon which my thoughts cried out in repetition.

Not only had my teacher successfully performed inception in my young, impressionable mind, but she also wrongfully punished me by making me stand in an outdoor hallway. It was not my exposure to the summer heat that angered my mother nor was it the school's failed attempt to send me back to kindergarten that made her blood boil. It was the question I asked her with a stream of tears rolling down my five-year-old face: "Mommy, is something wrong with my brain?" I cried as my voice trembled with defeat, and Mommy's heart was broken.

All the lessons she taught me about loving myself, being confident, and knowing that I'm fearfully and wonderfully made were suddenly covered in a blanket of doubt. With every fiber of her being, my mom assured me that there was nothing wrong with me. She went to war for me, asking God to not allow this seed of insecurity to be watered any longer. How many times has a parent, guardian, or loved one gone to war for you in your life?

As I share this story, I can't help but think of my son who, at this point, has been growing inside my womb for almost seven months. I can't help but to feel anguish at the thought of any parent or future parent facing a similar situation in which their child looks to them for reassurance. My best guess is that you ask yourself similar questions that I ask myself: What will I say to my son? I imagine that I will try to be a better version of myself, someone who is able to instill in him a sense of self-identity that combats the narrative others will try to write for him.

What I witnessed as a child was not always pleasant but, for the most part, it was a clear example of reality. And that's really the only example any of us need. I encourage you to reflect on the harsh life lessons you were once taught as a child, and how you came to accept reality for what it was: The reality that Mommy gets scared too or the reality that Daddy isn't perfect.

Throughout my teenage years, the blame game became my only source of escape. I began gaining lots of weight and blamed my father, who had been my track coach when my parents were still married but no longer kept me active and healthy. My grades were sometimes poor, so I blamed the standards of my performing arts school for expecting too much from me academically. Everywhere I went, responsibility chased me, only because I was determined to run from it. Fear was my friend, one who never required too much from me. Fear kept my virginity in tact past the age of eighteen because I never wanted to be like my peers who were plagued with heartbreak, STDs, and unwanted pregnancies.

My sophomore year of college was just as exciting as my freshmen year. I was active in music, my greatest form of expression, and had finally adjusted to a well-balanced social and academic life. This didn't last very long. Historically Black Colleges and Universities (HBCUs) are famously known for creating environments of profound, unapologetic, black resilience. Most of the professors and college staff are black, and holidays that celebrate black culture become a citywide event. But no one ever speaks on the social issues within the communities of such institutions. Many have turned a blind eye to the violence and culture of abuse that is prevalent even to this day, and no one ever believes that they will be on the receiving end of a violent act.

My reputation as the friendly girl from Las Vegas preceded me, although I doubt it was for the right reasons. Being one of the only people on a college campus from my city meant that I was often an automatic target for gossip, discrimination, and overall isolation. This, however, never stopped me from being the social butterfly that I was. I kept busy and active, involving myself in every mass choir my Seventh Day Adventist campus had to offer. I immersed myself in my communications major by taking on extra credit hours and involving myself in various clubs and organizations. My determination to belong, while never quite fitting in, was astounding. Not only had I established a name for myself as a promising musical talent, but I was thriving in my major and became known for my script-writing abilities. For the first time in my life, I was running full speed towards my responsibilities and embraced the woman I was becoming. Nothing could stop the progress I had worked so hard to make.

Being so far away from home had its perks. I was able to keep in touch with family, my mother was constantly sending me care packages, and I flourished in my freedom. But I also experienced the painful, unsettling feeling of homesickness; it was a direct and immediate connection that I lacked. I yearned for that lifeline, which could only be sustained through a family unit. Thankfully, God had already placed me in an organization that, over time, would prove to be the only family I'd truly need. Art & Soul was the best thing that ever happened to me. When I first joined, I was only a freshman and was completely unaware of the lasting impact the group would have on my life. We told stories through original poetry pieces, held scheduled meetings to sharpen our craft, and produced themed shows throughout the school year, blessing our peers with pure food for thought.

During the first semester of my senior year, Art & Soul was prepping to put on the most anticipated show and the first of its kind: "The Sex Show." Previous attempts to produce a show had failed, given the parameters of the topic. After all, we did attend a very conservative university where mandatory chapels were held every Tuesday to help reinforce our Christ-like values. Our group learned from mistakes and realized that the only true way to prepare for a show like this was to have active workshops during which we met and discussed our own personal experiences with sex. To ensure the tastefulness of our show, we included two members of faculty in our process. This would put our professors' worries to rest, as well as give them a sense of involvement in what we were trying to do.

I was extremely excited to take this on, although I had no clue as to what I would speak on. All I knew for certain is that I could not be happier to contribute my own personal experiences, if it meant inspiring others. With our show just days away, we held our final meeting to share stories, as well as come up with a decent order of performances to help keep the audience engaged. The last thing we all wanted was for our show to be taken as a joke, leaving room for immature hecklers to spoil the moment.

"Okay, let's all go around the room and share our stories." Our club president, a great leader, had no problem taking initiative when it came to getting us organized. We all followed his lead. One by one, each member shared their experiences. Some members dealt with having multiple abortions, some were virgins dealing with the pressure to have sex, and others shared their struggle with forming true connections because of sex. Then, there was me.

"Well, I have a friend who isn't sure if she was raped or not." This statement blurted out from my mouth like vomit. The silence in the room was deafening. I knew I wasn't making any sense, but without interruption, I continued my elaborate lie.

"Well, she went to a party and it was packed with lots of drunk students. It was so packed and loud in the house that no one would've heard her scream. It's as though the guys knew what they were doing, like they had done this before."

My eyes had become a pool of shame, my voice shrouded in agony. My bluff was transparent, and my new family knew that this "friend" I spoke of was really me. The women in the group began surrounding me with support, as the volunteer professor talked me through my story. I continued to share my reasons for keeping this a secret for over two years, and went on to share that I was able to fight the guys off. Because I was a virgin at the time of the offense, my attackers were unable to fully penetrate me. They, like many of my other peers, assumed that I was not a virgin and, to their disbelief, they struggled to penetrate me. Everyone's faces around me suddenly reflected an understanding of why I was so unsure. And then in one breath, the professor said, "Honey, you were raped. Rape is not the act of non-consensual sex in itself. It is the intrusion as a whole."

My decision to share my testimony with an over-packed audience never felt like my own. I am not the first person to endure such a college experience and, unfortunately, I won't be the last. I did not seek attention or sympathy, nor did I wish to be praised for my bravery. All I wanted was to let those who were going through a similar struggle know that they were not alone. Not alone in their confusion. Not alone in their hurt and shame. Not alone in being misunderstood. But life plunged me into a fast forward motion from that point on.

After leaving for winter break just before my twenty-first birthday, I never returned to finish school. My lack of focus, matched with unfulfilling curriculum and courses, made leaving school an easy decision. I soon had to accept that, without a definite plan or course of action, neither school nor any other endeavors would prove successful. I sought counseling so that I could get closure and, when that failed, I looked to other methods of coping with my new reality.

The performing arts had summoned my talents once again, so I allowed myself to be spread thin. I was starring in productions, directing, and writing scripts, all while working full time. Sure, I had conquered fear in some areas, but I still struggled to really tackle where fear shackled me the most. I appeared fearless to those who witnessed me perform, hustle, rehearse, and record music. Frequently, those who requested my services the most took advantage of me. "Are you still singing?" "I can't wait to hear your album." "When is your album coming out?" "I'm shocked you haven't made it big yet." Comments like these typically only come from those who don't support you, would never pay you for what you do, or have no knowledge of what measures you've taken to achieve your dreams. Blind obligation had disguised itself as my responsibility for a long time, only because I allowed it. Yes, I was drained, giving of myself to everyone around me. Feeling needed was addicting, but I was still left feeling empty.

But eventually, I dropped the extra weight in more ways than one. Most would say I was already an attractive young woman, but that never changed my desire to strive for my absolute best body goal. There was no denying my talent as a singer, songwriter, and performer, but I had lacked the drive to reflect my talents in a physical form. I took faking it to a new level and decided to actually become the change I was always destined to bring about. *Insanity* emerged to pull me out from my deepest low.

I remember feeling defeated. I set out to conquer an intense exercise routine and gave up after a mere twenty minutes on an hour-long workout DVD. My consistency felt inconsistent most days, but since this was my sixth attempt to complete the *Insanity* workout series, I figured I would at least give my best effort. Days turned to weeks, weeks to months, and before I knew it, none of my clothes fit me properly. One morning, my boyfriend and father of my first child looked at me and said, "Wow, you look super skinny!" Him calling me skinny was not necessarily the compliment in this case: The compliment lied solely in the simple fact that he knew how hard I'd been working to become fit and noticed my progress like everyone else noticed, before I myself was able to truly see it. My new and improved body instantly set the tone for my new and improved confidence. My direct messages on social media were flooded with requests for fitness advice from girls I attended college with. Never had I imagined that I would one day surpass them in the fitness race as the new "body goals."

My enhanced sex appeal came with new problems. As a female music artist, I have to be three times as talented, only to receive half of the respect of male artists. I faced the sexually driven stigma that comes with my "look." For example, most producers will simply correspond with a male artist through email and often never meet to complete records in a recording studio. As a female artist, I am almost always met in person and addressed with an inappropriate term of endearment (e.g., "sweetheart," "gorgeous," "beautiful," etc.). Then, there's the unwanted flattery and invitations to "come over and smoke," as if the only way I can receive a beat is to grace a male producer with my company.

Before I was forced to deal with the chauvinistic behavior of countless producers, one producer proved to be a great collaborator. However, our creative relationship was cut short when he relocated and took his talents elsewhere. Though, I was quite frustrated, I knew the only thing I could do was move on and never again rely on one person to help my vision come to life. As years went by, I experimented more with music. From getting great reviews to being posted on popular music blogs, I was steadily creating a powerhouse name for myself. But where there are triumphs, there will also be trials to test your faith.

On September 8th of 2015, I was involved in a dangerous car accident: The car I was in was hit multiple times by a drunk driver. The only thing that kept me and three other passengers alive was being inside a Dodge Charger. Had we been in any other type of vehicle that was not a muscle car, all four of us would have been severely injured, if not dead. After months of therapy and healing, I hoped my season of tribulation was coming to an end. I was wrong again.

In early December of 2015, I experienced the worst kind of discrimination a young, black woman could ever encounter in a Las Vegas casino. I was with a friend at a bar, enjoying drinks on the house, and had been carded by hotel security, which was fine the first time it occurred. The second time, I was carded by the same security guard and was met with unnecessary hostility, during which my arm was forcibly grabbed. As a past victim of rape assault, certain things can trigger a panic, leading me to feel the same emotions and fear I'd felt during my rape. I was grabbed again and then beaten unconscious.

When I woke up, a tooth was missing, the one next to the missing one was chipped, and my lips were busted. The cops were going through my belongings, looking for a reason to put fault on me, but nothing was found. And just like that, I became another statistical black body abused by authority.

My family, boyfriend, and close friends were all livid. "Why won't you fight this?" they'd ask. My attempt to fight it with my first lawyer had been short-lived, since he didn't have faith in my case and for understandable reasons: Every time the authorities abuse their honor to protect and serve, an ugly picture is painted in media about the skittles that were stolen three years prior or the fact that the "suspect" had previously served time for such and such reasons. Once again, I allowed my fear of past issues with the law to get in the way of my purpose and I ultimately became my biggest adversary. I have many regrets about how the situation could have been handled on my part, being the obvious victim. But what I absolutely don't regret is the newfound peace I've been able to keep, as a result of simply letting it go.

As I continue to live my story, I am still flaunting a toothless smile. Fear crept into my life for the last time, shortly after this incident. For a brief period, I decided to stop pursuing my passion of music. "I can't possibly move forward. How can I continue to sing, if I can barely smile? Who would I even appeal to?" For over a year, I convinced myself that restoration wasn't an option. But when you have a fire within you, a burning desire to be great, you must push forward. So here I am. Still going, still writing, and getting paid to do so. Most importantly, I run towards my dream, singing my heart out with a new song of resilience. The only difference between the woman I was then and the goddess I am now is that I have done away with fear. It took a long time to accept this journey, but I'll never allow myself to be out of tune again.

My SOARROARity™ Rules

Surrender: Let go of your past and accept that it made you better.

Omit: Get rid of any leftover fear or doubt.

Acknowledge: Those who have supported you, uplifted you, prayed for you, and gone to war for you must always be acknowledged.

Run: Run full speed towards your dreams. Run towards what scares you. Be brave.

Remember: Never forget the past, but focus on what events led to your lowest point and what brought you out of that pit.

Open: Be open to all possibilities. Never box yourself in.

Ask: A closed mouth is never fed, so ask for what you need. Can't hurt!

Risk: Be willing to take risks in order to get to the next step of your life.

SOAR~ROAR Reflection

1. What am I having a hard time letting go of?
2. What am I afraid of, and when did I learn to fear what scares me?
3. Who do I have in my corner?

4. What is my greatest passion?

5. What events led to my present circumstance?

6. What barriers do I need to break?

7. What do I need help with?

8. What am I willing to sacrifice, in order to achieve my passion?

AISHA MARSHALL

GREEN
I'm Not Pink

I grew up in the dusty city of Las Vegas, full of fields and deserts. Riding my dirt bike and being rough with the boys was fun for me. I was a guy's girl. Nothing made me happier than to hang out at my granny and poppa's house with my cousins (all boys) on the weekends. We would entertain ourselves for hours hosting our very own tag team wrestling matches up until something would break. Those days quickly changed once my mother started to ask me if anyone had ever touched me "down there." My answer was always "no" but my mother wasn't a fool. There was no more hanging out with my cousins.

I was my mother's only child, raised by my grandparents and completely sheltered. Though I was shut in with my family's overprotectiveness, I gained a lot of skills and street knowledge. I pretty much had to stay in a child's place. I could never ask any questions. All I would do was sit, watch, and listen, and maybe I would catch a crumb or two to use later on in life. In those moments of being by myself, I would get frustrated trying to comb the little hair on my baby doll's head. One of my aunts showed me how to use yarn like extension hair, and just like that, I was a nine-year-old braiding hair. I really didn't understand the difference between a gift, a talent, or a trade. I lacked the understanding of what it would take to be successful.

Our family was blended with many beliefs, such as, Christian, Jehovah's Witness, Muslim, and Seventh-Day Adventist, just to name a few. Morally speaking, finishing high school without a baby was an accomplishment. I played sports to keep busy and to stay under the radar. I was left home by myself most of the time so the television became my educator. I'd play my usual game of "Tic Tack" by myself, collecting ideas for the materialistic things I wanted. In school, I would never match in my attire. I loved to put together my "fits" that no one else would be wearing: Green sweaters, yellow pants, one long earring, one stud, and a pair of my granny's pumps. I became great at deflecting compliments because of my uncertainties and insecurities. Little did I know that, while I was asking questions like "Why do I have a gap in my teeth?" or "Why do I hate the color pink so much?" I had begun the journey to self-discovery.

Alone in the empty room with no one to ask me if I had everything I needed for my high school graduation day, my mind raced with thoughts of what I would wear under my gown. Will my cap fit over my weave? Does this green nail polish look good on my brown skin? I went to bed with rollers in my hair, but when I woke up, my set was not completely dry. I still had to pass out the tickets to the ceremony; only four out of the twelve invitees would be present.

I had gone my entire middle and high school years wondering where my father, mother, and grandparents were at my track meets and basketball games. But today was going to be a great day! My momma was going to see me walk the stage and I could showcase her to those who had questioned her existence.

While lining up in the back, waiting to be seated for the ceremony, all I could think about were the conversations that weren't happening in my household. Why did no one ask what my plans were after high school? Trying to tune out the happy chatter amongst my peers, the nervousness set in. Everyone was going on senior trips to Mexico or heading straight to college. I was getting my diploma, which was good enough for my family.

It was time. I walked across that stage and smiled, just praying my mother captured a good picture of me. The graduates made it to the exit where families get to greet their student. I heard someone shout my name.

"Aisha!" shouted my mother. "Let us see your diploma!"

I was so excited to snatch it out of the manila envelope trying not to rip it. There it read: *Certificate of Attendance*.

The look on everyone's faces, including mine, was priceless. We were all at a loss for words. Confused. And all eyes were on me. The questions started to come from all directions. "What does this mean, Aisha?" "Did you even graduate?" "You received all of your credits, right?" I mean have you ever been hit with this kind of news? Have you ever had to choose between being forthcoming or finding a quick lie to cover up until you could face reality for yourself? I wasn't prepared, even if I had received my diploma. The "What Now?" was my biggest concern because the show had to go on.

I later found out that I did not pass my math proficiency exam, which was a requirement in the state of Nevada. Honestly, this standardized test was like an epidemic for my class across the city. I thought this was a mistake. I had gone through school just barely passing, but never completely failing. I obtained all my credits and some from summer programs just to pass time. Was this one test going to be a determining factor to hinder my future? It was, because I allowed it to cripple me into believing that I was yet another statistic. Sure, I cried. I felt defeated, ashamed, embarrassed, and most of all, insignificant. But the worst of it was the uncertainty.

The negativity was overwhelming. "Oh Aisha, you won't be able to get a job without a diploma. You are going to have to get your G.E.D.!" "You might have to make beds or work at a fast food restaurant!" At the time, I wasn't sure if the advice given was the best advice or the only knowledgeable thing my surrounding support could offer me. I sat before my grandfather, who once couldn't read or write but worked hard to provide for his growing family. This brave old soul and my grandmother took me in after raising their own children. He taught me that giving up was not an option, and a strong work ethic and skill could produce a check, with or without the education. I had to pull myself together.

Still, I really couldn't understand the emotions that were flooding my mind. So, I bypassed my reality and began to party, drink, and even smoke. I mean isn't that what one does when she is defeated and having a rough day? It was easier for me to portray everything as being "all good" since very few people, only those who attended my graduation, saw what was in the envelope. Though I had many beliefs in my family, no one and I mean no one ever told me to pray. I simply learned to panic now and possibly repent later.

Just before receiving my *Certificate of Attendance*, I had dedicated my life to Christ and was learning a thing or two about trust and having faith and a prayer life. You couldn't tell by looking at my other coping mechanisms. In fact, I was still so heartbroken, that I decided to share with a then-client and now mentor and friend, Toni Ellis, about my setback. She encouraged me to keep trying and not to give up. I struggled to understand how faith really operated. What I did not know was that my first accountability partner was placed in my life. God used her to pull on me over time in ways no one else made me think was possible. It was clear that I needed her and she needed me, for iron sharpens iron!

Going back to the proficiency test, I went on to retake it a few more times but failed again. How many times have you found yourself settling because nothing changed in your situation? Did you consider opting out by saying to yourself, "This is just it for me"?

During my struggle to pass the test, the women at my church began to take me under their wings and mentor me through it. One of the sisters from my ministry let me work in her bookstore while another let me play in wigs at her wig store and assist customers. There it was, a yearning in my belly. Somewhere in my heart, I just knew there had to be more to me than just a back-up plan, but even filling out applications was so intimidating to me. I had no experience! I cried over every job that I didn't get and I still didn't have anything equivalent to a diploma. Through it all, I was optimistic for myself.

By faith, I plugged my ears to whispers of doubt and cut the strings of every stronghold that was attached to me, and I applied for positions that appeared to be out of my league. I went on to not only get the job I wanted but was nominated for Employee of the Month twice in less than ten months. I went from being insecure to gaining more confidence almost overnight. Promotion after promotion appeared to fall into my lap. I began to realize that I was on a path to breaking a cycle of generational curses.

Life and death is in the power of the tongue. Who was speaking life over me? Was I even speaking life over myself? Somewhere, I began to say, "I want more for myself! I deserve it!" I had to die in my emotions that had me paralyzed and be reborn in the endless possibilities that I didn't know existed. After all, I had always listened to family tell each other what they would not and could not have, and watched them embrace lack in almost every area of their lives. Have you ever witnessed this?

I went on to work many corporate jobs and dealt with the politics that came with them. I still did not have my diploma but I had become comfortable with the paychecks. Then, on one particular occasion, I had gone to lunch with coworkers and listened to everyone share about how much they made, and where they shopped and traveled to. That was when I realized that everyone seemed to be robotic. Programmed to believe that this was it in life: Work, pay bills, buy shoes, and do it all over again. And everyone seemed to be shacked up and tangled up in some mess. My then workplace was a soap opera and I too was starring in it, learning in real-time what I could and could not share, who I could and could not trust. I had to be reminded of why it was so important for me to get that diploma. Was it to be in this space to feel confused yet again? No!

God is always there but we run from Him. I was deep in my flesh and lust and everything else. When I began considering change, all those negative thoughts resurfaced: "Am I good enough?" "Do people really like me?" "Is everyone using me?" I felt alone, despite having my accountability partners—it was I who was not present. I felt as though no one could pull the good out of me because everyone around me was okay where they were. I still needed more; I needed redirection and clarity.

Not every moment spent on that job was a waste. While employed there, I met a young lady who I bonded with and who is still very present in my life. She was like the sister that I never had. She was educated. Because she had a hearing impairment, to some, she was considered disabled. However, to me, she was so fulfilled and I admired her strength and determination through her adversity. She, like Toni Ellis, pulled on me in that drama-filled workplace and encouraged me to go to beauty school. After all, between this sister friend and all of the drama, I was forced to reflect on what I really wanted out of life.

I loved wearing weaves, shopping in second hand stores, and most of all, doing hair. And I did it well! So, I spent some time searching for the requirements to attend beauty school. That year, I enrolled in an adult high school, studied the same test that I had failed several years prior, passed, and obtained my diploma! It wasn't that I didn't have other people around me cheering me on and encouraging me to go ahead and seek better choices for my life. It had more to do with *me*, not being able to see past the talk. All I knew was talk! I was great at it! The walking it out was the struggle for me. Doubt was always present because I really thought I was going to fail. I watched people around me start and stop projects all the time.

I then, by faith, quit my job and went to Cosmetology school. God provided. I was living in my first apartment, doing hair in my kitchen, and going to school. I remember driving my 1993 Geo Storm with duct tape on the driver's side window. It was then that I was given the opportunity to showcase as a student in a national hair show in Las Vegas. This had never been done before. Usually the beauty school may be featured but I was set apart. My resounding question was "God, what are your plans for me?"

After that show, I learned that word of mouth was everything. Clients were coming from all over. At one point, I even had to go mobile because I did not like the traffic at my house. My bills were paid. I lived on the West side in a slightly upscale, lower socioeconomic project apartment with three bedrooms, and my rent was under six hundred dollars. God provided.

I was offered to work on the set of two short film gigs booked through the school and started my journey in resume building. I even worked on the set of a music video featuring popular video vixens that I'd only seen on TV. All of this was just amazing, considering I wasn't even licensed yet! This all happened in beauty school thanks to testimony after testimony.

Are you starting to see a pattern? Delayed but not denied, and the favor of God was ever present. Can you recall the times God still showed up on your behalf but it appears you didn't deserve it?

But at some point, my faith grew weary, despite God constantly showing up for me. I was working, but I had upgraded my vehicle to a Jeep and my funds started to dry up. While experiencing the dry season, I volunteered to drive one of my little mentees, who I called "Little Sister," to her home in California at the end of her Christmas break. The entire drive down, I was adding up the gas I would have to spend to and from, and what would be left over to buy myself something to eat. I had all of sixty-seven dollars to my name going. Little Sister's mother was so grateful for my selfless act that she invited me to their church in Los Angeles for their New Year's celebration.

It was a mega church. On my way to the event, I counted that I had thirteen dollars left. I just kept praying and saying, "Lord, I trust You!" At the end of the night, we were walking down the church stairs when I noticed that this gentleman kept turning around and looking at me. He appeared to be talking to himself. By the time we got to the forum area, this same man gestured and nodded his head, and said, "Yes!" He then turned towards me and handed me a hundred-dollar bill. In that moment, I didn't care who saw or heard me. I shouted aloud with a praise of thanksgiving. Not just because I needed the money and I was nearly broke for real, but because God reminded me that my life has always been through Him and that He has allowed me to overcome so much! He allowed me to see that this story was already written about me. I just had embrace it and not rewrite it in shame. He blessed me with all of the creative things that made me *me*. To be set apart and loving the color green.

So, why do I love the color green? Let's define "green" and its meaning: Between yellow and blue in the spectrum, representing the color of life, renewal, nature, and energy. Green is associated with growth, harmony, freshness, safety, fertility, and environment. And this is what the color green means to me: I had to get my feet wet by the blues while swimming in the waters of life. Burned by the beaming ray of the sun on the surface of my skin, I had to see if I could handle the challenges I would face.

To be faced with every type of uncertainty was a huge threat to me. I was displaced from my cousins, abandoned in a home filled with family, tone-deaf to the heartbeat of my gifts growing inside of me, and left mourning at the crossroads of life after graduation. Every layer of doubt that I dressed myself in each day had me blind to my God-given purpose. God never intended for me to suffer long. I had to learn to trust Him and respect the process in finding self and breaking cycles.

This SOARROARity™ means a great deal to me because I never had the sorority experience in my education. But today, I am a SOARROAR! I am in this space, filled with green, always seeking growth and being renewed. I had to find my safety, not just in God but in the acceptance of self. I'm extremely different and sometimes unfiltered. I didn't just have to find my way and a place to be positioned in, I had to create them.

I'm an innovator, a creator, an eclectic—and that's why I'm not pink!

My SOARROARity™ Rules

SURROUND yourself with people who pour into you. Toni Ellis coached me through life, long before she began doing her work professionally. She has been a constant support, sister, and friend.

OPERATE in faith, not fear. Having to trust in something you've never seen before is difficult, but when you do, it's something so beautiful.

ACQUIRE the knowledge you need to move forward. Stop talking about what needs to be done and just move on it. Time doesn't wait on anyone!

REINVENT yourself and thrive. Acknowledge the dead weight of what's holding you back. Accept the you that you can see and soar.

REARRANGE the people and their positions in your life. Outside of God, no one comes before you.

My SOARROARity™ Rules

OFFER no apologies! Period!

AFFIRM yourself when no one else wants to cheer you on.

RESIGN from the activities that do not have anything to do with your forward movement.

SOAR~ROAR Reflection

1. During your life experience, have you ever felt like you were alone, without family or friends?

2. What color best represents your extreme high of life? Why?

3. Outside of your job, what activities make you the happiest?

4. In what season of your life did you find yourself holding back some hidden truths?

5. Who is your biggest supporter?

6. Have you ever been uncertain? Explain.

7. Would you consider your style eclectic or simple? Why?

8. How does it feel to know yourself?

TOSHA RONE

THE HUXTABLE EFFECT
It Was All A Dream

> "We must be willing to let go of the life we planned so as to have the life that is."
>
> —*Joseph Campbell*

As usual, I looked fly as I got ready to hop into my pearly white Denali to pick my kids up from school. Flawless and the finest Mama in the school, you couldn't tell me nothing! I was doing the damn thing. My husband was a surgeon, I was a lawyer, and our four kids were a triple threat: Gifted, gorgeous, and athletic. We were seemingly perfect and had the house, cars, fame, and fortune. When we stepped out, all eyes were on us, The Joneses. Couldn't nobody keep up!

As I was getting ready to head out, the doorbell rang, echoing through the house and my memory. I answered the door. A gentleman stood there.

"Are you Mrs. Jones?"

"Yes."

"Mrs. Jones, you have been served."

It was a court order for my husband, Jeff, to undergo a paternity test. It stated with specificity whom he had sex with (some white bitch's name) and when they had sex. My head started spinning. I didn't know if I wanted to scream or cry. I needed a minute to hit the pause and rewind button on my life.

Let's hit rewind first: My loneliness as a child was consumed by watching *The Cosby Show*, a hit TV show in the late to early nineties that revolved around the Huxtable family, an upper middle-class black family, father a doctor and mother a lawyer with five children. I was obsessed, eyes glued without blinking, when I watched the show. My mother worked long hours to support us, and my father was nowhere to be found. I felt abandoned by him and desperately wanted a family just like the Huxtables. This obsession ignited a fire within me—I decided I was going to do everything to create a family just like theirs and that's exactly what I did.

I married my high school sweetheart. In my mind, we were going to be the first in our family to become college graduates, as well as a doctor and a lawyer. I actually envisioned our faces transplanted onto the bodies of Cliff and Clair Huxtable. That probably sounds sick and twisted, but I was on a mission to fulfill my childhood obsession and dream. I signed both of us up for college—whether Jeff liked it or not, he was going. I attended school, worked full-time, and supported our growing family while Jeff finished college and medical school. After he graduated, I attended law school and he attended residency. We had four kids in tow, with one in diapers. I was a sleep-deprived, Red Bull-drinking, multi-tasking mama. I know it was God who literally picked me up and carried me through law school. I never would've made it without Him.

We ended up graduating at the same time. Jeff accepted a prestigious position as a surgeon, making over half a million the first year and over a million the next. The money was rolling in. We did it! We made it! Life was going along as planned. We had it all and a beautiful family to match, three handsome boys and a beautiful little girl. We replaced the Huxtables with the real-life Joneses. And so the Huxtable Effect was in full gear. But that dream was crushed the day the doorbell rang.

I thought this particular affair was behind us. When I confronted Jeff about it, he claimed it was a lie, saying his accuser was trying to set him up so she could get paid. But that was a real lie. I literally thought I was on *Maury* when Jeff called to tell me the results of the test. It had come back 99 percent positive: "I am the father." Surprisingly, I wasn't angry or ready to kill him. I later learned I was in complete shock, equated to experiencing death.

I walked around dazed and confused like a wounded soldier, stabbed with a million invisible arrows. The saddest thing about betrayal is that it never comes from your enemies. Jeff's DNA was flowing through the life of a child that wasn't mine! This was some pain! It burned a whole through every ventricle of my heart. As I was burning inside, Jeff acted like it didn't faze him. He told me I wasn't going anywhere or divorcing him. I couldn't believe the arrogance of this SOB! I immediately filed for divorce.

Signing Day

As I began signing my divorce papers, tears poured from my eyes as the faces of my children and our lives replayed over and over in my head. At this point, Jeff and I had been together for two decades and I felt like I was a quitter. Quitting is not in my blood. My family and I were born winners! This home-wrecking hoe was not going to ruin my family and shatter my dreams. I left the soggy divorce papers on the table and decided to save our marriage.

We attended martial counseling and signed up for a couples' retreats. Our pastor prayed over our family and home. Our parents were equally devastated and prayed that we hold it together. I renewed my relationship with God and sought personal counseling to hold my broken self together. On the outside, I was beautiful; on the inside, I was shattered in a million pieces.

It takes two, but Jeff wasn't putting forth any effort to save our family. He eventually stopped attending counseling and church, and showed no interest in either. So I did what I did best: I prayed. My prayer was specific: "Lord, do I continue to try and make this marriage work? Or do I divorce him? Please make it clear and make it plain." As I waited for the Lord's answer, I noticed Jeff getting comfortable. He thought he had won me back and his life could go on as if he just hit a speed bump along the way. However, God had a different plan.

God started to reveal things to me the day I found pictures of Jeff's baby boy tucked away in a dusty old book. The face of this beautiful, innocent baby made my heart skip a beat. Could I accept him? I immediately thought, yes, of course! Although his conception hurt me like hell, God showed me that I had enough love in my heart for him. He was a gift.

A Predictor of Future Behavior is Past Behavior

A few months after I decided to save my marriage and accept our bonus baby, Jeff and I planned a trip to Chicago to attend one of his medical conferences. This would be a perfect getaway for us to spend some quality time together. However, a day before we were set to go, our sitter cancelled and I was unable to go. As soon as Jeff arrived in Chicago, we got into an argument over something trivial. While he spent a week in Chicago, we barely spoke.

When he got back from Chicago, he immediately plopped down on the couch and fell asleep. As he lay there snoring, I watched and wondered: How could he act like nothing bothered him, while I was still wounded? My intuition was telling me that something just didn't feel right. I felt God nudging at my spirit. "Speak to me, Lord."

A few days later, Jeff came home early and laid his cell phone on the kitchen counter. Our inquisitive son liked to play games on Jeff's phone and quickly discovered some pictures. With anxiety in his voice and shock on his face, he asked who was in the picture with his dad. I looked and did a double take, but quickly dismissed the woman as one of Jeff's patients. My son looked at me with a blank stare, as if he couldn't believe I was lying to him. These were provocative pictures of Jeff and a blonde, time and date stamped during his trip in Chicago.

Unbeknownst to Jeff, I strip-searched his phone and found more pictures. Every picture was another stab in my heart. I flew into a rage! I said "That Mother—(you know the rest)" and "Thank you, Jesus" in one breath. I sent the pictures to my phone as evidence and laid his phone back on the counter as if nothing happened. For the next two weeks, I put on a plastic smile. I checked his cell phone records every day. He called a mysterious phone number in Chicago on his way to work and the same number on his way home. At the two-week mark, I called the number and a woman answered. I found out that she met Jeff while he was in Chicago. They hooked up, had sex, and she claimed that she had no idea he was married with a wife and kids.

In an effort to receive a full confession from Jeff, I asked him to meet me for dinner so that we could discuss some issues concerning the kids. At dinner, I asked him about Chicago and whether or not he met a woman while he was there. He immediately got defensive and said, "Here we go! I thought we were past this stuff and here you go with your craziness!"

I told him to swear to tell the truth on the lives of our four children, and I named each of them. He swore on our children's lives that he hadn't met anyone in Chicago. In my Maury voice, I said, "That's a lie!" I laid out the pictures of him and the other woman. With this sinister smirk on his face, he looked at the pictures and said, "That's not me. I've been set up!"

I was done! I gave him two deuces, strolled out of the restaurant, and never looked back

Divorced—Now What?

As much as I tried to pretend that everything was okay, my eyes told a different story. Eyes are the windows to the soul and my soul needed intensive care. My sister saw right through the brokenness and invited me to her church. I knew that the only way to get through the pain was by the grace of God. As soon as I entered the church, I experienced an overwhelming sense of comfort from the inside out. It was the Holy Spirit. While there, I wept like I've never wept before.

This was God's way of cleansing my heart and soul from the inside out.

To this day, what damages me the most is the pain that this divorce caused my children. My oldest son was the most affected and is still trying to cope. All I ever want to do is bottle up their pain and drink the poison that robs their souls. Because my love for them runs deep beneath my soul, I continue to struggle with this part. I don't know if this part of me will ever heal.

My SOARROARity™ Rules

*Girl! Put Your Big Girl Panties On: Eight Ways
I Healed and Moved On*

As my relationship with God strengthened, I didn't ask God to take me out of the storm. I asked Him to hold my hand and walk me through it. He not only held my hand but He picked me up and carried me through. I got through and so will you!

1. **Struggle**: The struggle is real. Every hurt has its own story, and so does every healing. My situation felt like a hit and run. I was in a state of shock: Numb, dazed, and confused. I struggled to get out of bed, eat, think, and sleep. I remember my little girl would make me tea, turn on the Disney Channel, and rub my head so that I would feel better. I was in a thirty-day coma.

Then one day, I heard birds chirping outside my window. I started to awaken, wiggling my hands and feet, grinning then smiling. Then, I heard the pitter patter of my children's feet running down the hallway. I popped up and all I heard was, "Mom's up!"

The state I was in was unavoidable and I learned that it was okay to struggle, just as long as I didn't stay there. Trust the struggle because, without it, you won't stumble across your strength to move on.

2. **Open up**: My heart was wounded and I kept it open until it started to heal. I aired it out by talking, shouting, and writing it out. I wanted to understand it head-on and not ignore the feelings so that it wouldn't continue to resurface. My Christian counselor, mom, and family were all on speed dial. I was fortunate enough to have them help me through this. I then surrounded myself with whatever brought me comfort (music, the Bible, warm baths, soothing blankets, and green tea). This was a turning point for me. I could've chosen a temporary fix with drugs and alcohol, but God and green tea got a hold of me. My wounds healed and scars began to form.

Open up, then express and acknowledge your pain. Don't be ashamed of the scars that life may have left you. A scar shows that the hurt is over, the wound is closed, you endured the pain, and God has healed you.

3. **Accept what happened**: I had to accept the fact that we were not going to mimic the lives of the Huxtables. Their lives were make-believe and ours were a reality. I wasn't the first or last woman whose husband had a bonus child. I accepted this, took a deep breath, and asked God to help me let it go. Every now and then, I revert to self-pity, feeling sorry for myself for what I didn't have and what I lost. But through counseling, I learned the five-minute rule: I set a timer for five minutes and, in those five minutes, I have a pity party: Cry, kick, scream, and throw a toddler tantrum. When the timer goes off, I must snap out of it and move on. It worked, and look at me now!

4. **Recognize:** I recognized what role I played in the demise of my marriage and family. I cannot place all of the blame on Jeff. We were teenagers when we started out. I didn't meet my biological father until I was fourteen, and growing up without him had a tremendous toll on my ability to love myself and my ability to even know what love was from a man. I never experienced those and experienced abandonment instead.

    So ultimately, I was inexperienced in love and the concept of marriage. I didn't know how to love Jeff. Recognizing the role I played allowed me to replace the anger and bitterness that I felt toward him with compassion and peace in my heart.

5. **Rewrite your story:** I burnt a hole in Mary J. Blige's "No More Drama" CD. It was on repeat while I had mini MJB concerts in my car. That song was my anthem and I was rewriting my story. I also read a lot and wrote my thoughts in journals. Through this, I gained more understanding into who I am and what I wanted for my life. Exercising my mind and thoughts on new and positive things took away thoughts of my past. After all, my past is what I went through, it's not who I am; it helped shape me, but it does not define me. The key to getting over past hurts and trauma is to let go and no longer allow it to have power and control over your life. As my girl, MJB says, "I don't know only God knows where the story ends for me, but I know where the story begins. It's up to us to choose whether we win or lose, and I chose to win." I chose to win for myself, my children, and all the other young women who will come after me.

Re-writing your story requires that you take an honest look at yourself and where you may have blamed other people or circumstances for the way your life turned out. Think of the gifts that manifested as a result of it. For me, I wouldn't be the woman I am today if I hadn't gone through the pain. I wouldn't have been able to forgive my father and have a relationship with him today. And Jeff's son is a bonus and a gift.

You can't change the past, but you can change how it affects you. When you put a positive spin on your past, you can redirect your future. It's a story that you can rewrite.

6. **Offer forgiveness:** Let's talk about the f-word. Forgiving a man who wasn't sorry seemed impossible. But forgiveness *is* possible. If I didn't forgive, I wouldn't be able to leave the past where it belonged—in the past.

   The first person I had to forgive was me, myself, and I. I was angry with myself for taking Jeff back after he repeatedly cheated on me throughout the marriage. So why did I stay? I was taught to forgive for better or for worse. Once I got honest and forgave myself, I was able to forgive Jeff and my father.

   Don't get it twisted! Forgiveness does not make what was done right. It just means that I'm letting it go, giving it to God, and letting Him decide what the consequences of Jeff's actions are. By forgiving, I unshackled myself from the chains of anger and resentment. I taught my children the power of forgiveness and love. Maya Angelou said, "Forgiveness is the greatest gift you can give yourself." That is so true; it gives the gifts that money can't buy: Peace, love, and happiness.

7. **Aid someone else:** I thought I'd never get to a point where I'd help someone else go through the pain of infidelity or divorce. When I'm able to help, counsel, and/or comfort someone through his or her pain, it also heals my

soul. Maya Angelou also said, "When you learn, teach. When you get, give." I've helped many through prayer, compassion, understanding, and a listening ear. Not only did I rescue them, it helped heal me.

8. **Rejuvenate:**

    - *Mind, Body and Spirit*: Rejuvenate means to look or feel younger, fresher, or more lively. Practicing yoga along with meditation rejuvenates my mind, body, and spirit.

    - *Mind (Meditation)*: I was working a high stress job at a demanding law firm. My blood pressure would climb as soon as I pulled into my parking space. Meditation was my answer. I would take a break midway during the day to put some headphones on and find a five-minute meditation exercise on YouTube. Just a few minutes a day made a huge difference in my life. Take a deep breath, relax, and meditate.

    - *Body (Yoga)*: I was a fast food junkie and was dehydrated from not drinking enough water. I was at my heaviest weight and my blood pressure was through the roof. I needed a long-term fix and was introduced to yoga. Yoga saved my life by transforming my mind, body, and sprit. I look and feel amazing! However, I get it— not everyone is into yoga. Get some type of physical fitness (walking, running, Zumba, etc.) on a continual basis to get your body moving. Watch your life change! *Spirit*: I have to fuel and feed my spirit daily. It is what drives my inner peace. If I don't, it's similar to going on a hunger strike: "The fruit of the spirit is Love, Joy and Peace" (Galatians 5:22). I do this by fostering my daily, personal relationship with God: If your mind is ruled by the Spirit of God you will have life and peace (Romans 8:6). I was willing to let go of life as planned, so now I'm truly free to live the life that exists for me. I thank you, God.

SOAR~ROAR Reflection

1. Which of these SOARROARity™ rules are most beneficial to you and why?

2. Which rule do you struggle with the most?

3. What did you take away from this story of forgiveness?

4. What is your story? Have you ever thought about rewriting it?

5. What type of rejuvenation do you want to experience?

6. For me, it was the Huxtables. What fantasy do you need to let go of for the sake of forward movement?

7. What steps will you take toward rewriting your story?

SHARDÉ EDWARDS-DAVIS

THE POWER OF VULNERABILITY

The Journey to Understanding and Valuing Strength in Vulnerability

I wasn't meant to write this story for my personal gain; I was meant to write it for the exact person reading this book. The one who is struggling with something that she "thinks" is bigger than her. The one who is questioning existence and her purpose here on Earth. The one who wonders, will she ever be seen, understood, or enough? Yes, we all have been there. I am here to share my story and what helped me make it through…victoriously.

This was initially a story of sorrow and victimization. I felt I deserved to be heard, seen, and recognized for all the wrong I went through, and this chapter was going to be my platform. The world was going to know my story, my fifteen minutes of pity from the masses. I was hurt and went through a lot. Why should people not feel sorry for me? Why didn't those who knew me feel bad for me? Why didn't anyone pity me and let me wallow in my sorrow? Was I not worth the empathy? It must be because they don't care about me, right? I dealt with favoritism as a child, as well as the feeling of being a burden to my parents. I was cheated on and mistreated. I was stabbed in the back by so-called friends. I didn't get enough attention. That qualified me as a victim. I deserved my pity and I planned to write all about it.

This book happened at the perfect time. It had been three months since my dad and I talked after we had a silly argument because of miscommunication and pride. When we tried to reconcile, or at least get back on track, our similar personalities once again crashed and I found myself storming out of the conversation with tears in my eyes and him leaving my house. The question of us talking again was never clarified.

This was the perfect time for me to share my story of childhood woes; how I didn't get "the perfect treatment" as a child. I wrote an entire three pages about how I felt mistreated; but, when I read back through it, I felt silly. Do not get me wrong: Some of the things I dealt with as a thirty-one-year-old woman were wrong, but what I had to remind myself of was that God gives His strongest soldiers the toughest battles.

I then thought about you again. So, I had a "come to Jesus" talk with myself and realized that pity was not why I went through what I went through. We all have battles, obstacles, falls, and wars in life. The one thing that I got from my reality check with myself is that this is not about me; it's about what I do with what I've been through and how I can help the next person, either preventing them from making the same mistake or showing them how to get up after some of life's nasty falls.

"Challenges are gifts that force us to search for a new center of gravity. Don't fight them. Just find a new way to stand."

—*Oprah Winfrey*

"Shardé, you are so strong!"

I learned to resent this compliment growing up. I didn't want to hear that. I wanted to hear how they understood my pain and would pity me. But why I did feel this way? I couldn't answer that question. Then, I dug deeper. Being a victim got you attention. It got you resources growing up. My family focused on the more dependent and poured into them. So, as the strong one, I didn't get the attention I felt was deserved. As a child, I got this concept but never understood why.

As an adult, I began to strongly question the reasons why. I wouldn't call it resentment but I strongly started to question, "Why was the dependent seen or heard more than the ones who were doing well?" I used to say, "Well maybe I should go ahead and drop out of school or act up, and maybe someone will feel bad for me." I knew in my heart of hearts that that wasn't a reality for me and my independence was just a part of life I had to accept. In fact, my answer to why I was not doted on was there along and I chose to ignore it: "Shardé, you are so strong!"

As a child, I struggled with the lack of attention, but then I realized something: I never told my family I needed that attention. I just assumed they should know. I never expressed my desire to have them show up and be supportive as I felt they had been for others. This was a big issue I dealt with (and am still dealing with), the issue of being vulnerable. At the time, I didn't know what to call it or what it was but I knew it was something I had to avoid.

If I had asked for more love, it would have come off as desperate or attention-seeking or, worst of all, jealous. I didn't want that to be my story. I desired a closer relationship but never knew how to go about it. I built a wall so thick to prevent any hurt or rejection. I didn't like the feeling of feeling weak or vulnerable. I started to connect the two. Vulnerability = Weakness. At a young age, I learned to protect myself from being rejected before I even gave myself a chance to see the power behind vulnerability.

vul·ner·a·bil·i·ty (noun):

*the quality or state of being exposed
to the possibility of being attacked or harmed,
either physically or emotionally.*

What I thought I could do was numb my feelings of rejection, sadness, and fear, never realizing that I would end up numbing all emotions. This began the start of a roller coaster ride of a life because I didn't know who I was. I wore a mask to protect me from others but what I missed out on was being my true, authentic, and real self. I missed the opportunity to be seen, the very thing I was seeking in the first place.

I married my best friend of fifteen years in October 2016. After a long time of being friends, we decided to be more and one thing led to another and we walked down the aisle. Before my husband and I got married, we went to our premarital counselor together. Both of our parents were divorced and had never remarried; so unfortunately, we didn't have the best example of marriage to follow. We were going into this sort of blind. At this time, divorce was at an all-time high, and we were in the era of the side chick and sugar daddy. Although we didn't have perfect examples to follow, we agreed on one thing: We needed to see a premarital counselor. We wanted to build the foundation of our relationship on solid ground.

We both work in marketing for the mental health field, but even with so much education on afflictions and the importance of mental health, walking in to see a therapist of our own was a very new experience. As we waited in the lobby for our therapist to come out, I have to admit, I was a bit embarrassed. I remember looking around in the lobby and seeing who came in and out. A part of me wanted to blurt out to every person, "We are only here for pre-marital counseling." Even in that moment, where I should have been gracious to be there with my future husband, I found myself trying to set a good perception. No weakness over here. I remember burying my head into my phone and hopping on social media, so I could escape the possible stares and the need for me to justify my reasoning of being in a therapist's office.

We finally got into her office, sat on her comfortable couch, and then waited for her to start. We had no idea what to expect, so we kind of sat on separate ends. I think we both had things on our mind we wanted to discuss that would make ourselves, individually, look better. I believe we went there with the intent to prove that the other person was "wrong." We started out with an assessment, went through a couple of questions, and discussed a few things. In the session, the counselor was quiet and poker-faced. She never shared any emotions when we told her a story about the relationship. At the end of the session, she told us our homework: To look up the meaning of each other's names and to treat one another based on the meaning of that name.

It seemed like an odd request but I am not a licensed therapist, so I went along with it. Aaron and I had been arguing a lot since he moved to my city. We had a lot on our plates: We had just started living together after dating long distance for two years and were realizing that we didn't really *know* each other. He had left his baby girl back where he'd come from, my daughter had to be introduced to a new man who was not her dad, and we had a wedding to plan, coordinate, and pay for in less than ten months. Again, we had a lot on our plates.

Still, we went home after our first session and did our "homework."

Aaron's name: A Hebrew baby name, meaning lofty, exalted; high mountain. Biblically, Aaron was Moses' older brother and keeper by God's command. He was first high priest of the Israelites, remembered for the miraculous blossoming of his staff or rod.

Shardé: As a girl's name is pronounced shar-DAY. It is of Yoruban origin, means "honor confers a crown." Phonetic variant of Sade. Associated with the crown or queen.

This one exercise blew our minds. The counselor wanted us to see who we were meant to be and that the way we were treating each other was not of our namesake. It also pointed out how we were acting toward ourselves. It was powerful to see our names written out and put together.

> "A good name is rather to be chosen than great riches, and loving favour rather than silver and gold."
>
> —*Proverbs 22:1 (KJV)*

My soon-to-be husband wasn't getting the best of me because I wasn't recognizing my own worth. A name can't get much more royal than Shardé and everybody but myself saw that. My namesake says I am strong, but I was seeking pity from others. It wasn't that others didn't feel for me or didn't care; they just could see the power and strength inside of me so they trusted me. They saw me tackle obstacles and overcome issues for myself and others with dignity, love, and passion. They saw the strength in my stride and were awed by it.

God blessed me with strength, optimism, an amazing aura, and resiliency. He blessed me with the ability to soar and, through this exercise, I was able to overcome all of the hardships I faced. It was in that moment that I decided to change my narrative. I was no longer going to play the victim, but only act in my God-given right as the victor!

Our premarital counselor continued to be great. She opened our eyes to so much. At one session, she requested that I come alone. I was certain that she was going to tell me how to deal with my soon-to-be husband and help him become a better man, but I was mistaken. She wanted to address something she'd seen in me. In fact, she could see a lot of herself in me. She reviewed my pre-session assessment, a questionnaire that all patients fill out prior to her meeting. I was skeptical about filling this out because this was also a lead sheet we used for my nine to five. As I mentioned, I worked in marketing at a major mental health hospital and we would use these forms to fill our hospital. If we saw certain boxes checked, we would follow up with patients, offer free psychological assessments, and check them into our private inpatient hospital.

I filled out the assessment but wasn't completely honest. I didn't want to come off as "crazy" or needing additional help. Besides, I knew that my fiancé was the "issue," if anything. But when the counselor and I began this one-on-one session, she immediately reviewed the sheet to guide the flow of the meeting and set the tone. She told me what type of woman she saw in me. I am a "tell me like it is" type of girl and she understood that, so as I would talk, she would refer back to my assessment and say, "Well, you said you weren't feeling this way." This went on for about fifteen minutes. I was being fact checked and it was very hard for me to hear that. I didn't want to be labeled as having anxiety, being stressed, questioning myself, or feeling less than. I wanted to come off as strong and put together (Oh, the irony). She called me out and then said she wanted me to watch a short TED Talk.

I love TED Talks so I was all for it. This particular presentation was by a well-known author Dr. Brene Brown, titled "The Power of Vulnerability." I sat there thinking I would breeze through it and then discuss what she wanted to discuss. I am good at holding educated discussions, so I was happy to talk about things in detail. As she mentioned earlier, the counselor saw herself in me, so she sat and watched as well. I thought I could drown out the movie by looking at my phone or gazing out the window but she demanded that I was in tune.

I watched the entire twenty-minute talk and saw so much of myself clearly defined. I realized at that moment, my issue was one of vulnerability. Before this, I never put a title to it or a definition. I just didn't want to be perceived as weak, and now I understood why. I was afraid of being vulnerable. This TED Talk hit me like a ton of bricks and my therapist knew it would. She asked me to go home and review my notes and journal about my feelings, vulnerably. To take the time to really learn about vulnerability and the meaning behind it.

I learned in my review that I numbed vulnerability due to fear: Fear of rejection, pain, sadness, etc. I wanted to be in control of how I was perceived and weakness was not one of the emotions I wanted to show, ever. According to Dr. Brown, vulnerability is defined as uncertainty, risk, and emotional exposure. It is to let ourselves be seen, deeply seen. It is showing our true authentic selves. To be vulnerable is to love with our whole hearts, even if there is no guarantee of getting the same in return. It means to practice gratitude and lean deep into joy, especially in moments of fear. It is to believe passionately and be fierce about our lives while being grateful. Most importantly, it is believing we are enough.

It was everything I wanted and I couldn't believe it. Everything I desired was on the opposite side of everything I taught myself to be and how I wanted to be perceived. To be vulnerable meant that I would stop screaming and controlling, and start listening. I would be kinder and gentler to myself and to the people around me. It was this life I was after and it only meant I had to take off my mask and be myself. I didn't just want to overcome this struggle. I wanted to soar.

I then desired to roar when I decided it was time to change this narrative.

Being vulnerable is living brave daily. I believe I am on the path to being able and willing to express my truth no matter what. It is showing the essence of my core, opening my soul, and letting if flow. I believe I was tasked with this to allow others to see themselves in me.

What I dealt with in my life, the challenges I faced, are all valid. I struggled with shame, unworthiness, and the disease to please, but I also recognized my strength, resiliency, and power to bounce back from each situation. I am now working on the best version of myself to not only soar but also roar!

When you mask your true authentic self, you don't allow others in at all and you become who they want you to be. I had to take off that mask and be *me*. I defined my idea of happiness and started to live it. I went against what society, family, or friends wanted for me and said it's time for me to live for me. This was an inside struggle because, when you live with a mask, armor, and shield all your life, defining happiness is hard. I had to get to know myself all over again. I had to fall in love with myself and love all over me! This was the best part and it went hand-in-hand with defining my happiness. I learned what I liked to do and what I needed for me to be my best version. I learned the concept of keeping my cup full—not only full, but overflowing. It was like dating someone who knew all my "spots" and that is an amazing feeling.

But the most important step for me was to align myself with my higher power. For me, that is God! My heavenly Father is mind-blowing and *so* good to me. I learned how to pray and meditate on His word. I am not where I need to be but I am working on it and so grateful for my growth. I celebrate His word and live by His will for my life.

I now only accept and expect only amazing things, opportunities, experiences, support, and love. I speak beauty over my life and recognize when something is not going well so that I can turn it into a lesson from which I can learn. I accept the beauty of the lesson and the new level I am about to move up to. This process came easier and more fluidly when I began reciting my daily affirmations. Do you recite affirmations? What is your favorite affirmation that gets you all powered up and ready to go daily? Mine is: "I expand in abundance, success, and love every day, as I inspire those around me to do the same!"

I wake up and, before my feet hit the floor, I recite this affirmation. I got this affirmation from one of my favorite books, *The Big Leap* by Gay Hendricks. I absolutely get fired up when I say this. It helps me realize my worth, importance, and purpose to serve others. This affirmation is one of many. I usually recite a variety but will tweak it based on my current needs and desires.

I learned to trust, appreciate, and love. Moving towards your best life is truly a journey and it needs to be valued. My path to vulnerability is nowhere near over; in fact, I am at the very beginning. But I am blessed beyond measure to be on it at all.

On this beautiful journey, I believe what has helped me the most was developing my rules of success. I suggest you develop your own on your path to soaring.

My SOARROARity™ Rules

Surrender: I surrendered to the idea that being vulnerable is powerful and a strength versus a weakness. I became in tune with my feelings, wants, and desires. I try to push myself outside of my comfort zone daily to increase my ability to surrender to the zone of vulnerability.

Obedience: I became obedient to His will for my life. I am trying to stop myself from controlling everything. I became still and started to listen.

Awareness: I recognized the issue and didn't blame others anymore. I realized that I can't fix anything in my life if I don't become aware of the problem myself.

Recognize Your Worth: I recognized that I was enough as I am today. I stopped searching for perfection and just gave the best of what I had. Those who were truly meant to be connected to me would do so naturally.

Radiate: I decided to radiate. We often hear that people dim their light to help others feel better about themselves. That is not being authentic or true to yourself. You are placing yourself on the back burner, and then, in my case, expecting someone else to put me back on the front burner. It doesn't work that way: You must show others how you deserve to be treated and radiating the self is one of the ways!

Optimism: I remain optimistic. I believe life is beautiful and I am going to live as beautifully as I want my soul to be. I decided not to allow the negativity of others to bring me down. For me, living optimistically is saying thank you to my Father.

Authentic: I decided to take the mask off. If you can't accept that I sometimes need help or I am not superwoman all the time, then you are not meant to be in my circle anyway. Those who are rooting for your rise will support, love, and uplift you!

Rejoice: Celebrate yourself! Early in my story, I discussed my need to be celebrated. Well, what's wrong with celebrating yourself? This also goes back to showing people how you deserve to be treated. One of the ways to rejoice is self-love. Take the time you need to ensure your cup is full and overflowing!

SOAR~ROAR Reflection

1. What is your definition of vulnerability?
2. Have you struggled with vulnerability? If yes, when?

3. What is your idea of living bravely?

4. Who on your support team keeps it real with you and loves you through it?

5. What was one of your toughest falls?

6. What action did you take to get up from that tough fall?

7. What are your SOARROARity™ Rules?

8. Why is this important to you?

ABOUT THE AUTHORS

Toni T. Ellis, Soul Sparker and Clarity Coach, mentors emerging thought leaders into becoming published authors. She offers clarity to the one with clouded judgment, focus to the one in disarray, and action plans to the one in need of specific steps to execute lofty ideals.

As an author, Ellis' books serve to encourage women and girls to discover, accept, and embrace the true essence of their purpose. She has self-published two books: *Baby Girl's Mirror* and *God's Dowry for His Daughters: His Good Treasure,* and she co-authored two Amazon bestsellers: *Bold is Beautiful* and *Fabulous New Life*. She believes her soul was purposed to serve others in their pursuit of self-development, self-discovery, and self-love. Ellis holds a Bachelor of Science and a Master of Arts in Education.

Learn more about becoming part of the SOARROARity™ and joining the next volume of books at www.tonitellis.com

Deanna Cummings, affectionately called Dee by family and friends, is mother to three sons, grandmother to two grandsons, Reigning Queen of her domain, encourager to all, and a prayer warrior who believes whole-heartedly in the power of prayer.

Cummings is a part of the Owens Law Firm team, who specialize in personal injury, civil, and criminal law matters. Additionally, she is a certified notary and a volunteer with the Hayward Unified School District at Tyrell Elementary, where she encourages her fourth-grade little ones to soar.

In her spare time, she enjoys writing poetry, hosting family affairs and weekend get-a-ways with her girls, and baking Deelicious Desserts. However, her greatest joy is sharing the good news about the greatest love of all, Jesus Christ, her Lord, Savior, and Deliverer from captivity.

Learn more at deanna@mowenslaw.com

Ronda Bailey, the "Bounce Back Queen," is an entrepreneur, speaker, and an author. As a survivor of childhood sexual abuse, she is passionate about empowering women to break free from pain so they can live an abundant and purpose-filled life. She shares her story of overcoming hardships to become better instead of bitter in her upcoming book, *She is Resilient*.

In 2017, Bailey founded Speak Out and Shift, a non-profit organization dedicated to increasing the conversation and awareness around sexual abuse and assault to understand why so many survivors choose to remain silent, and to promote encouraging environments to speak out and dramatically make a shift to end the social stigma for victims of abuse. Speak Out and Shift also connects women and their families to resources that will help heal and strengthen survivors.

Bailey currently resides in Oklahoma City with her husband and their youngest daughter.

Learn more at www.RondaBailey.com

Jocelyn L. Wallace is an entrepreneur, philanthropist, marketer, and author. Her purpose in life is not only to survive but to thrive. A resident of Las Vegas, she is often referred to as a social butterfly. With more than twelve years of experience in marketing, she's worked in radio, television, and a few top billing and advertising agencies in Las Vegas. She has also consulted, managed, and provided marketing services to clients within the travel and tourism vertical, lifestyle and entertainment vertical, and community and government affairs.

When she is not out networking or doing "marketing things," Wallace enjoys serving the community and providing marketing services for non-profit organizations such as Broadway in The Hood and A Woman's Foundation, which she co-founded.

Contact her at Jocelyn.Wall7@gmail.com

LaShonda Mobley is a licensed professional counselor, author, actress, worshipper, vocalist, songwriter, and therapist from Oklahoma City, Oklahoma. In 2010, Mobley received a Master of Education in Applied Behavioral Studies from Oklahoma City University, where she graduated Magna Cum Laude and was awarded Who's Who Among College Graduates. She is a mother of three children, and her motivation and drive are inspired by her children and the desire for them to achieve greatness. Mobley's greatest inspiration comes from a deep desire to give back to God and His Kingdom as He and so many others have imparted into her life in miraculous ways. A scripture she stands on is Jeremiah 29:11: "For I know the plans I have for you," declares the Lord, "plans to prosper you and not to harm you, plans to give you hope and a future" (NIV).

Learn more at www.lashondamobley.com

Tamara Omondi is a native of El Reno, Oklahoma. She is the owner of Boots to Bowties Event Center, Nelson's Catering Co., and Streamline Events, LLC, all based in Oklahoma City. She is also the founder and CEO of Sox of Love, an organization that collects new cotton socks for children and teens in foster care, the elderly, homeless men and women, and our veterans.

Omondi graduated from Northeastern State University, where she fostered her first love for music performance. She uses her mezzo-soprano voice to heal the broken, give hope to the hurting, remember the forgotten, and to simply be His light. Her mission statement is, "To create opportunities for people to intentionally spend time and make memories with those they treasure most."

Learn more at www.tamaraomondi.com

Kindra Lowery is an innovator, motivator, mother, and trailblazer. Having raised three daughters of her own, she now enriches the lives of other children through fostering and mentorship. As a community strategist, she strengthens communities, one child at a time, placing them in a position to thrive. Professionally, she has also been a corporate liaison. Her attention to detail and passionate pursuit of excellence resulted in her elevated profile with several entities.

Volunteering in a managerial capacity for a myriad of non-profit organizations, Lowery's desire to impact the lives of women has been abundantly realized. Organizing feedings, clothing drives, and counseling sessions are but some of her work with her community.

Learn more at thetransparentpen@gmail.com

About the Authors

Ashley Q. Tillman is a native of Las Vegas, Nevada. She attended the University of Nevada, Las Vegas, where she majored in Communications and Accounting. She now works as an accountant for the state of Nevada and also advocates for the importance of home ownership as a licensed realtor. She gives back to her community as a mentor and donates her time to organizations such as Common Tree, Three Square Food Bank, and the American Cancer Society.

Through her work life and social involvement in the community, Tillman gained a "can do" spirit and is always open to new ways to better herself and those around her. She is a co-founder of A Woman's Foundation, a nonprofit organization that empowers and uplifts women. Through her organization, she develops programs, events, and resources with the mission to provide positive platforms that award women in their communities and give them the opportunities to be their best selves.

Learn more at aqtillman@gmail.com

Tianna R. Lewis is no stranger to creativity. With a passion for songwriting, she has committed her talents both on and off the stage. In 2008, she graduated from the Las Vegas Academy of Performing Arts and International Studies, where she majored in Theatre. Her appreciation for music and script-writing grew while studying Communications and Classical Voice at Oakwood University.

Having starred in and served as assistant director in a number of *Broadway In The Hood* productions, Lewis has also spent many years volunteering at the West Las Vegas Arts Center Performing & Visual Arts Camp. She has attributed most of her rearing to this camp, which she attended in her younger years and first fell in love with dance. Her intuitive writing skills have given her the opportunity to continue working closely with the arts center as a key scriptwriter.

Learn more at tiannarlewis@gmail.com

Aisha Marshall has been styling hair since she was ten years old. She has developed a reputation for excellence in hairstyling among her family, friends, and the surrounding urban community, and has won several titles at local hair shows. She earned her Cosmetology license in 2009 and went on to continue her studies under Patrick Bradley. She exposes herself to current hair trends by traveling abroad as well as to popular trendsetting U.S. cities such as New York, Los Angeles, and Atlanta. She demonstrates her ability to do hair, makeup, and wardrobe daily, and is committed to empowering women through beautification one head at a time.

To contact Aisha, email her at Amstyles2012@gmail.com

Tosha Rone is an attorney, business consultant for start-ups, real estate investor, people connector, and mentor to many. Through her personal struggles and failures, she uses her experiences to mentor others to reach their true potential and to live authentic and whole lives that balance mind, body, and spirit. She does this personally through daily meditation and yoga.

Rone is a single mother to four children and an adoring "glamma." She loves to travel and splits her time between Las Vegas, Nevada and Denver, Colorado.

Find out more at www.ToshaRone.com

Shardé Edwards-Davis is a passionate event professional, marketing executive, and business development strategist. She has garnered over ten years of hands-on experience in holistic marketing management including corporate relations management, marketing communications, events management, and strategy development. She is a graduate of Johnson & Wales University with a Bachelor of Science in Marketing Communications.

Shardé currently resides in Las Vegas with her husband, Aaron, her daughter, Leah, and their soon-to-come bundle of joy, Prince Landon. When she is not working within her full-time job as a mom and an advocate for supplier diversity and women-owned businesses, she is running her own upscale wedding and event planning business, Shardé Janine Events, LLC. She is an avid reader and a strong believer in prayer, self-care, and self-love, and is dedicated to promoting the message of living a life you love and loving the life you live.

Learn more at www.shardejanine.com

CREATING DISTINCTIVE BOOKS WITH INTENTIONAL RESULTS

We're a collaborative group of creative masterminds with a mission to produce high-quality books to position you for monumental success in the marketplace.

Our professional team of writers, editors, designers, and marketing strategists work closely together to ensure that every detail of your book is a clear representation of the message in your writing.

Want to know more?
Write to us at info@publishyourgift.com
or call (888) 949-6228

Discover great books, exclusive offers, and more at
www.PublishYourGift.com

Connect with us on social media

@publishyourgift

www.ingramcontent.com/pod-product-compliance
Lightning Source LLC
Chambersburg PA
CBHW071614080526
44588CB00010B/1134